issues OF conscience

issues of conscience

LAUREL T. HUGHES, PH.D.

Bridge-Logos *Publishers*
Gainesville, Florida 32614 USA

Issues of Conscience
Dr. Laurel T. Hughes Ph.D.

Printed in the United States of America
Library of Congress Catalog Number: 00-107091
International Standard Book Number: 0-88270-797-3

Published by:

Bridge-Logos *Publishers*
P.O. Box 141630
Gainesville, FL 32614, USA
http://www.bridgelogos.com

Contents

Dedication

Preface

Section I – The Sanctity of Life

Chapter 1 **The Value of Life and Death**
The Old Morality
The Treasure
Honoring Motherhood
Can I Forgive Myself?

Chapter 2 **Abortion and Genetics**
"Unusual" Circumstances
A Bloody War
Life and Justice
The Value of One Life: Joni Eareckson Tada
Vigil on the War Front

Chapter 3 **Life Awareness in Other Nations**
The War in the Womb
Civil War
Theology of Euthanasia
The Legality of Euthanasia
Caring or Mercy Killing?
Israel for Life

Chapter 4 **Compassion and Science**
Truth or Consequences?
Giving Up Your Life
Shouting at Evil
Lucinda's Story
Compassion: David Reardon

Section II – Biogenetic Realities

Chapter 5 **Life for Sale**
A Word From Pearl S. Buck
Awash in Death
Human Genome Project
The Nuremberg Trials
Karen Ann Quinlan
Patents on Humans
Brain Death and
Euthanasia

Chapter 6 **Ethics Revisited**
"Non-Treated" to Death
Living Wills
The Twilight Zone

Chapter 7 **Genetic Engineering Is Here**
Testing and Abortion
Artificial Reproduction
To Do or to Die
Breeding for Beauty
Truth and Genetics

Chapter 8 **To Clone or Not to Clone**
Genetically "Perfect"?
Is an Embryo a Human Life?
Full Speed Ahead

Section III – Asia, Model of the Future

Chapter 9 **Atrocities in Asia**
A Corporate Confession
Land of the Free, Home of the Brave
China's Beautiful Babies
The Asian Girl-Child
Prayer for the Girl-Child
Godly Leadership

Section IV - Life Issues Professionals

Chapter 10 **Legal Concerns**
Global Courting
Keeping the Treaties
Addicts and Experiments
The German Legacy
The Third Reich and Today
"Rare and Safe"?

Chapter 11 **Human Rights and Active Faith**
The Sale of Human Rights
Religious Persecution
Comfort Zone of the West

Chapter 12 **Medical Ethics**
The Dark Side of Medicine
A "Technological Spirit"
"Active Help in Dying"
A Baltic Battlefield
What About Prenatal Testing?

Chapter 13 **Medical Activism**
A Study in Dignity: Dr. Francis Schaeffer
The Hospice Movement
Reducing the Pain
A "Pool of Dreadfulness"?
Pharmacists: Unlikely Crusaders Doctoring Death
South Africa Speaks Out
Assisted Suicide

Chapter 14 **Biblical Family Planning**
Emergency Contraception
What Are Abortifacients?
A Birth Control Holocaust
The Family-Centered Approach

Section V - Strategies for Life

Chapter 15 **Methods for Activism**

The Coming Collision
Media Infiltration
Dr. Death
A God-Defying Act
How to Become an Activist
A Prayer for This Age

Chapter 16 **Activism Around the Globe**
A Call From the Families of the World
Great Britain
Northern Ireland
Australia and New Zealand
Zimbabwe
The Vatican

Chapter 17 **Closer to Home**
They Called Themselves Fishermen
Nehemiah at the Wall
The Gates of Hell
Enlightening the Clergy

Section VI – Heroes of the Faith

Chapter 18 **Testimonies**
Smiling Fascism: Charles Colson
A War on Compassion: Kurt Dillinger
Sidewalk Counseling is Really
Evangelism: Joseph Scheidler
The Hand of God: Bernard Nathanson,
M.D.Thankfulness Might Mean Life:
KeithTucci
Empty Playgrounds: Norma L. McCorvey

Extremism: A Hallmark of Christianity:
Randall Terry
God's Way, in God's Timing: Kay Arthur
The Last Word

Appendix A **Contributors**

Appendix B **Human Rights Organizations**

Appendix C **Global Networking**

Dedication

You shall not murder. (Exodus 20:13)

Your hands made me and formed me; give me understanding to learn your commands. (Psalm 119:73)

Issues of Conscience is lovingly dedicated to our adult children, **Bethany Laurel** and **Jonathan Gordon,** whose birth mothers gave us these two priceless gifts to know, to cherish deeply, and to love for many years on earth with an eternity in heaven to enjoy. The blessing of the next generation they produce is the continuing miracle of life that this book has endeavored to convey.

And it is dedicated to all of those you will read about who have put their faith to the test in the struggles between good and evil, life and death, that which does not fade away and that which does. Some of their names are found herein, but thousands more through the ages will never be known except to the Trinity—and to us, when we meet in glory.

Issues of Conscience is dedicated to those who have gone before us in centuries past and those sitting in prisons now for their acts of obedience and bravery. They are saving lives, both physically and for eternity. These are ordinary people with an extraordinary love for Jesus Christ. They may be just like you who have decided to identify with His sufferings—as did the first martyr, Stephen, and twentieth century believers like Betsie and Corrie ten Boom, Dietrich Bonhoeffer, Martin Niemöller and countless others without a name on this earth. Thank you for having lived honorably before the name of the Lord Jesus Christ in the cold and cruel world to which you were born.

Finally, I salute those who will read and be changed. For your new contributions of character and love, for exposing your hearts by instructing the weak, for learning to go and give, for beginning to rescue life by calculating the high costs.

Thank you all for bringing life to the dark corners.

Preface

I wish we had a disclaimer for this book: "Not to be Read without Parental Supervision." Shocking as it will be, we will probe the heart of the science of life and death.

Genetic research is a multibillion-dollar industry that most Christians never encounter, outside of the few who will do almost anything to obtain a child. To begin this journey into the dark side of research, you will have to do more than call your parents, lock the doors, and fasten your seatbelt; you'll have to take the wheel in developing an enlightened ethical view of what the bold "new" future holds for humanity.

What does God have to say about "moving the ancient boundaries"? We need to consider the biblical and moral position on organ transplants, for both the donor and the recipient—and the buying and selling of human tissue and living organs that this process entails. And we need to grasp the excruciating pain felt by tiny pre-born babies as young as eight weeks-old, babies who are dismembered part by painful part and thrown into the cash registers of abortionists.

As you read, you can expect God to develop your conscience in areas you may be totally unfamiliar with or even unaware of. It is better to turn back now if you feel you lack the raw courage you'll need to finish reading this book.

Issues of Conscience is not intended to frighten you, but it does provide a fresh opportunity for you to face the reality of a world willingly caught in its unquestionable final days.

And you will be inspired.

Just what *can* one person do to make a difference? You will see many examples in this volume. Many will make you weep. Your understanding will expand immensely. You will connect with others in different countries who love and serve the Lord.

You will forever appreciate the devotion to diversity with which God operates in all He has created, how He wants it to function, and why it only works *His* way. You will meet the warriors, each clothed distinctly by race, gender, age, class, nationality, and even by their spiritual gifts and the funds available to them to complete the tasks God has called them to do in their sections of the battlefield. It is an adventure into a new world.

And now I want to give you a short view of the adventure ahead.

Do not hand over the life of your dove to wild beasts. (Psalm 74:19)

The young woman on the cover illustrates the utter hopeless despair of this age. She is not a victim. She is a planned event. She represents multiple millions of us who are targeted through manipulation and misinformation to be numbed into compliance with powerful agendas, long set in motion. We see the shreds and tatters of shattered lives strewn through world wars, planned poverty, derailed reproductive schemes, false messiahs, and fragmented families.

We act like children at Christmas, dazzled by the bright lights, the tasty food, the false period of cheer and goodwill that evaporates the very next day. We smell the fresh green tree, shake the gaudily wrapped gifts, and make supreme "sacrifice" and effort to provide a one-time trinket to the most obscure of acquaintances. After an exquisite banquet, we pat our full stomachs and nap again, oblivious of what is happening in the ghettos of the world. Oh, that all of life was like Christmas Day!

May I tell you that there are no "Christmas Days" left?

Heaven is reserved for heaven. We are still on the battlefield, and there are casualties, known comrades, all about us. We must ascertain who the Commander-in-Chief is, what His plans are, and how they are to be carried out to get off this planet alive. We also know that the enemy is supremely clever at undermining our spiritual capacity to identify him in all his guises and understand his purposes.

Issues of Conscience is a trumpet call.

It is a redirecting of the corps's focus to recognize and interpret what is happening on the battlefield, and further, what strategies and methods can be used to properly equip yourself to not only *not* become a statistic but also to effectively outwit and overcome the enemy.

You cannot live anywhere and not be impacted by all that happens beyond your property lines. Life issues pass through your doors when a crisis hits in real life—from before birth with an unwanted pregnancy to old age and on into death—with life-defeating medical care. It doesn't matter what the problem is; life is now "for sale."

You'll notice that we seldom use the term "pro-life." That term has become too narrowly associated with abortion to fully convey the breadth of this book's subject matter. Instead, we will also use the term "life issues" to include human rights violations, physician-assisted suicide, euthanasia, fetal tissue research and sale, biogenetic engineering, DNA manipulation, human cloning experimentation, and more.

All are life (and death) issues. Our task will be to recognize the morality of each, because the Christian is responsible to both understand the error of man and uphold the integrity of *imago Dei* (the likeness of God).

Beginning with **Section I—The Sanctity of Life**, we lay a brief foundation for biblical and ethical reasoning. What is the value of life? Who is now setting the parameters on experimentation with life that fails to distinguish between snow peas and rats and human beings in terms of their value?

Secular ethics, fueled by curiosity and promises of monetary gain, has made massive inroads into biblical ethics. Unless we are clear on what God's boundaries are, we will blissfully cross the line to the other side.

Can we stop at the line? If so, do we gaze adoringly across the abyss between God's will and Satan's desires, hungering after "treasures" that dangle within plain view? Unless all human life is held sacred, fetal tissue research makes sense. "After all, the baby *was* aborted. Why not use its tissue if it could help someone else?" You might not yet know God's answer to this subtle rationale, but you will.

Is there justice for all? Does one tiny life, no matter how impaired it is—as Joni Eareckson Tada comments on—have intrinsic value?

Finally, in this first section you will learn about technological wizardry. Having a godly ethical base will mean an extra measure of obedience, especially in cases such as sterile couples who decline to use scientific methods for obtaining that much-desired baby. Should people be cloned? What about gene splicing and evolution? Do you make a living will or allow God to determine your final moment of life?

Section II— Biogenetic Realities details many of Satan's death traps. We'll look at secular philosophies that cause us to deviate from "the way" after we've accepted "the truth and the life." You'll see the hand of God in Revelation as well as the fist of Satan.

Victims of Satan's fist speak out and fight back in a powerful way. This level of bravery from all over the world is refreshing. These activists stem the tide of death, holding out the mercy of God to free the captives, so they can know and love God with purpose.

Section III—Asia, Model of the Future will lift the veil on Asia, the future model of death. For people in that part of the world, there is a conspiracy against the unsuspecting and impotent. But even with its people control and population control, is China any worse than "enlightened" Western nations that murder their young with planning and funding? What is the West doing about the repressive and fast-moving flood of girl-child slaughter in parts of Asia?

Section IV—Life Issues Professionals includes five chapters on understanding the legal and medical implications in the global fight for life. Lawyers, legislators, parliamentarians, doctors, nurses, pharmacists, and medical staff have had much success in repealing laws that are flawed. They recognize—up close—the ramifications that unimpeded access to death has on their private morality.

After a look at biblical family planning, **Section V—Strategies for Life** outlines and illustrates doable and practical strategies to enter the battle at all levels. There are thousands of methods for activism in all types of life issues. You will see a handful of examples of activism, from congressmen to United Nations lobbyists to human rights fighters to praying grandfathers.

And finally, in **Section VI—Heroes of the Faith**, you will meet Chuck Colson, Kurt Dillinger, Joseph Scheidler, Bernard Nathanson, Keith Tucci, Norma McCorvey, Randall Terry, and Kay Arthur, whose special essays highlight their unique giftings with regard to the value of life.

Issues of Conscience is structured to provide you with a breath of fresh air between heavy encounters with immorality and its consequences. You will eavesdrop on personal electronic mail (e-mail) transmissions that fly into outer space and back down, then across seas and continents. You will read my mail!

Please bring an open mind and a pure heart.

We all know that living on planet Earth is no easy assignment. But take comfort in knowing that our days are short while we await Jesus Christ's soon appearing. We are not here to waste time in gaining worldly wealth and vain success that will evaporate with the funeral service.

Asaph, the great psalmist of David's day, looked around and saw "the prosperity of the wicked," who seemingly had no struggles. Could it have been because they "went with the flow" of the world system? They didn't have to fight the current by going against it or being pushed over unseen waterfalls onto slippery rocks below.

Asaph must have wondered, *Why are the righteous continually in jeopardy with no funds, ill from endless kingdom work, and often misunderstood among their peers?* This is how he expressed it in Psalm 73:

> Surely God is good to Israel,
> to those who are pure in heart;
> But as for me, my feet had almost slipped;
> I had nearly lost my foothold.
> For I envied the arrogant when I saw the prosperity of the wicked.

They have no struggles;
Their bodies are healthy and strong.
They are free from the burdens common to man;
They are not plagued by human ills.
Therefore pride is their necklace;
They clothe themselves with violence...
Their mouths lay claim to heaven
And their tongues take possession of the earth...
When I tried to understand all this,
It was oppressive to me
Till I entered the sanctuary of God;
Then I understood their final destiny.

We do know that God resists the proud and that the wicked wear pride as a necklace! They are proud of being proud! But who can withstand God, resisting you and all you do?

We must agree with Keith Tucci to be thankful in all places, in all things, and with all disadvantages. This means submitting to and maintaining dependence on Him to "work the miracle, make it happen, save the lives."

Let us therefore review history, examine the issues, understand the technological gurus, and recognize maniac scientists, medical research companies, and abortionists who profit from the sale of life. We want to discover their philosophies and agendas. If they are not stopped, their morally unfettered human experimentation will engineer a cold and godless world for our posterity. We form our own ethical mores if we are to succeed in preventing this.

If you take nothing else away from reading *Issues of Conscience,* take this:

Know that there is none like God. None.

We are but privileged creatures of His handiwork, with stewardship responsibilities in this war of holding all life sacred.

Later, by God's grace, comes the reward.

Section I

Sanctity of Life

Chapter 1

The Value of Life and Death

"Without a standard, there could be no justice; without an ethical absolute there could be no morality."

—David A. Noebel

People around the world are crying out for life. Cries are heard from China to Cuba, from Sudan to Sri Lanka, and from smaller, less-familiar places around the globe.

The people of these nations have demonstrated against injustice. They've petitioned their governments and the United Nations, and sometimes managed to have laws passed successfully. Meanwhile, other people were forced to give their lives for freedom and liberty. Their fight is for the right to live unharmed and unexploited in their own homes and villages.

When we ignore the violations of the more powerful over the weaker, life is allowed to disintegrate. It happens child by child, segment by segment. One small, abusive act of authority aggregates over time until the magnificence of life is caught and held captive.

* * * * *

Is life sacred, awe-inspiring, highly esteemed?

If so, who sanctioned it as sacred?

And who—or what—causes life to become trivialized, persecuted, and eventually stamped out? Will those of us who live in the lap of freedom protect and elevate the value of human life by actively resisting the wanton taking of it?

The church has learned how to feed the hungry, clothe the poor, provide shelter to the homeless, heal the sick, deliver from the demonic, and bring salvation. But have we learned how to bring righteousness and justice to the oppressed?

"To some degree, man has the [moral] law written in his heart and possesses, until he successfully destroys it, a conscience that brings guilt to his soul, which violates that law."

—C.S. Lewis

Injustice is rampant and diverse: children forced into slavery and prostitution, young women subjected to bride-burning, the pre-born subjected to horrific, excruciating, and fatal dismemberment.

What about the family provider who is unjustly rotting away in prison, or people whose bodily organs are stolen and sold over the Internet for profit?

In the struggle between life and death, we often don't know which side we are on until tragedy or the shadow of death cuts across our path. It could come through an unwanted pregnancy through the rape of our daughter, or a family member in irreversible pain, a son with a drug habit, an elderly grandparent tormented with dementia, or a disabled friend crying out for physician-assisted suicide.

People make life and death decisions every day—somewhere, some time. What are we, as a society, to do in the sticky places of life?

The Old Morality

For Christians, ethics is grounded in the character of God. "Made in God's image" encompasses the totality of a human being, not just the spirit or the soul or the body.

There is no new moral code, nor is there a possibility of there ever being one on this Earth—because God, as Creator, imbued each human *at conception* with His divine moral code.

"One of the distinctions of the Judeo-Christian God," said Francis Schaeffer, "is that not all things are the same to Him."

That, at first, may sound trivial, but it is one of the most profound things one can say about the Judeo-Christian God. He exists; He has a character; and not all things are the same to Him. Some things conform to His character, and some are opposed to it.

So those talking about establishing a new moral order are talking pure nonsense, because all morality originated from God's character. This is evident in the general revelation of God to Adam and Eve and their offspring hundreds of years before Moses set down the Ten Commandments. Cain knew immediately that he had broken one of God's moral laws when he fled in guilt after murdering his brother Abel.

The conscience that is placed within us at conception is a reflection of God's very character. It is that which the Apostle Paul referred to as "the work of the law written in their hearts, their conscience." In this sense, it is the "old morality," because it is the original morality and inescapable even to secularists.

Many factions claimed to have instituted a "new morality." Communism, for one, had a strict moral code, which Stalin mastered. Killing more than sixty million of his own citizens was moral to him, because his worldview encompassed the notions that "the many is more valuable than the few" and that the end (a New World order) justifies the means (mass murder). Any effort short of obtaining that goal would have been immoral to him and his henchmen.

"The human mind has no more power of inventing a new [moral] value than of imagining a new primary colour, or, indeed, of creating a new sun and a new sky for it to move in." —C. S. Lewis

---

The Christian ethic is revealed both through the general revelation (conscience and nature) and the specific revelation (written and spoken). Here again, C. S. Lewis brings the concept into reality:

> "The Moral Law...this Rule of Right and Wrong, or Law of Human Nature or whatever you call it, must somehow or other be a real thing, a thing that is really there, not made up by ourselves. And yet it is not a fact in the ordinary sense, in the same way as our actual behavior is a fact.
>
> "The task to Christianity in finding its moral compass is to determine what conforms to God's character and what does not. Then we will have an unshakeable opinion of what the sanctity of life is."

We all know that there is, in fact, an order outside of our five senses that compels us toward noble action. The voice of conscience speaks to us from millennia past to respect life, honor parents, don't cross forbidden lines, love God and neighbor—because things simply go better when we do. The most obscure culture that has no idea of what a Bible is incorporates these morals. It is the oldest of moralities.

"Ethics is based on ethical laws that reflect the very nature of God." —Norman Geisler

---

When we know God's character of justice, holiness, mercy, love, forgiveness, kindness, and truth, we have stepped into a high moral order. Abortion, euthanasia, addiction, donor fertilization and genetic predisposition—are these merciful, just, and kind, bearing truth within them to all concerned? No. They all fail the test of God's nature.

Modern and ancient morality are only distortions of the reflection of the Old Morality. There is nothing new under the sun, just aberrations of what God set down from within His character.

God's standard cannot tolerate evil, because everything positioned outside of Him is evil. Each person has an evil, sinful nature—but one that has His moral character stamped into his or her consciences. In this lies the conflict.

It is up to us to see our sinful condition, reject it, and gladly accept Him along with His will and His ways. Those of us who have done so should never fall for the imitation moralities abounding on the planet.

"No truly authoritarian government can tolerate those who have a real absolute by which to judge its arbitrary absolutes and who speak out and act upon that absolute." —Francis Schaeffer

---

When we wholeheartedly stand on God's side, we become a bone of contention to those who will not—and most who are in charge of nations will not tolerate our morality.

Worldview expert David A. Noebel states it like this:

> "For the Christian, God is the ultimate source of morality, and it is nothing short of blasphemy when we place ourselves in His role. And yet, if one does not submit his nature entirely to the moral absolutes founded in God's character, logically the only ethical authority residing over mankind is our own impulses.
>
> "It is important for the Christian to understand the fallacies of secular ethics, so that he can avoid the inconsistencies of unfounded ethical ideals. All secular ethical codes are an aberration of God's code and should be recognized as such."

The morality of the Old Testament was as much of God's revealed will as He felt necessary in those generations. When sin was rampant, God took action by sending a flood and fire from heaven; by destroying Babylonian gods, scattering people and confusing their languages; by giving the Ten Commandments; through war, exile, captivity into servitude; and through prophetic utterances and other diverse means.

Then God sent the person of Jesus Christ to settle the sin matter along with ushering in the eternal. Matthew chapters five through seven contain Christ's explicitly stated moral code.

We are to love ourselves so we may know how to love others with God's brand of love. But the church is confused about how to do this, and so its leaders meet together to resolve their own questions about how to be the expression of Christ to the world.

However, unless we get beyond our church walls and into the world to meet its social, physical, and spiritual needs, we have failed in our purpose on earth. The "social needs" are the ones we most falter on, finding it easier to translate Bible passages, provide food and shelter, and teach God's benign ways. But social issues are what life is all about. Seeing what they are and actively joining in is to bring the character of God into life's hellholes.

There is duty involved in knowing God. Norman Geisler sums up for us what that duty is: In serving God, we are found serving others.

Briefly stated, the Bible teaches that it is morally wrong to exploit the poor and morally right to help the poor. Whether the need is for food, clothes, or shelter, the believer is morally obliged to help fill the need. In fact, what one does for the poor, he does for Christ.

"For I was hungry and you gave me something to eat, I was thirsty and you gave me something to drink, I was a stranger and you invited me in, I needed clothes and you clothed me...I tell you the truth, whatever you did for one of the least of these brothers of mine, you did for me." (Matthew 25:35-36, 40)

How more naked, needy, and unsheltered can someone be than when they are abruptly and violently taken from the sanctity of the womb, unprepared for independent life?

Our God unequivocally defines moral obligation to His children: It is the carrying out of His character. His character is found in His many names, by which humans can understand and obey Him more clearly. Jesus is "the way, the truth, the life."

If He is life, then all human life is placed in a sacred domain. To destroy innocent life would be to distort the very image of God and, by default, create a new morality outside God's standard. How you perceive the whole right-to-life issue is based on how well you know God.

Where are the strong in this struggle, and what are Christians to do? In the following section, you will see what they are doing. Some things are small and doable. Others are nation-changing. Remember that Madalyn Murray O'Hair was only one woman, but one who changed America. She single-handedly had prayer to the Judeo-Christian God removed from public schools.

By the efforts of this one person, the slippery slope to cultural, civil, and social disintegration was shaped. Children now bring guns to school but are not allowed to bring God. So one person can make a difference, for bad or for good, for life or for death.

Now to my e-mail. I received the following correspondence from a woman who learned the value of life through a personal encounter with God:

The Treasure

"Not long ago, I found myself going through a dark time and sinking into the swamp of discouragement and negative thinking. It seemed to me that I had nothing to offer God, other believers—not even the world around me. Everything I touched turned to mud. Then one morning I happened upon this verse in the Old Testament, and the door of my heart flew open! I am alive and a treasure. And not just any old run-of-the-mill treasure, but God's *personal* treasure.

"Of all the people on earth, the Lord your God has chosen you to be his own special treasure." (Deuteronomy 7:6)

"How do we take that? When we perceive something to be a treasure because of its cost, beauty, life, and value, how do we treat it? We keep it in a special place and handle it very gently with great respect. We 'treasure it,' savoring the times to spend enjoying it. We want to show it to others and allow them to share in the joy too.

"Can it be that God looks at *me* with that kind of emotion?

"Yes, yes, yes!

"Not only am I His special treasure, even

more incredibly, He chose me for that position! It didn't just happen by some strange quirk of nature or accident of birth.

"I am a valuable treasure to Him, made in His image and, as His chosen treasure, I am set apart, a holy, chosen treasure of God, the Almighty! How can we question our value or purpose? It is true that life gets heavy at times, but the difficulties, the times when we feel buried in mud, are not what we should focus on.

"No matter what daily discouragement or failures have to be faced, we have unquestionable value, because we are the chosen treasures of God."

—Carolyn S. Larsen, Wheaton, Illinois

Honoring Motherhood

The following report on the work of just one activist shows the impact a single individual—submitted to the will of God and obedient to His calling—can accomplish.

"Patte Smith...congregation in rapt attention as she told how the Lord led her into sidewalk referral counseling...We were privileged to be prayer warriors and eyewitnesses to God's miracle rescue of Sheneika, a young pregnant teenager who was dragged to a clinic by her desperate mother. Patte gently called to her, and before anyone knew what was happening, the girl jumped into Patte's car, and her mother and Patte followed! They were taken to a crisis pregnancy center for help. A fine baby girl was delivered about four months later."

"We thus learn from scriptural revelation that human life possesses uniqueness, sacredness, or sanctity not possessed by other kinds of living beings. Thus, human beings are declared to be 'made a little lower than the heavenly beings and crowned with glory and honor.' By granting patents in human body parts, patent regimes revalue human beings...a form of biological slavery."

—C. Ben Mitchell, Patenting Life

"Sadly, there are now five clinics in the Orlando area with more than 12,500 babies killed last year alone. People come from all over the world, spend a day at the local attractions, and slip over for an anonymous abortion.

"Quoting another voice in the anti-abortion fight, our own Bishop John Howe, 'It does no good to condemn abortion as a sin if we're not going to provide an effective Christian alternative.'

"He spoke of changing the law, concluding that either 'America is going to bring down

> the abortion industry, or the abortion industry is going to bring down America.'"
>
> *—John and Pat Horner, National Organization of Episcopalians for Life*

* * * * *

One of my very best and long-standing friends is Linda McCollum. Our families belonged to the same church in the 1960s, and just before she and her husband, Jim, went to South Africa as missionaries, my husband and I set out for Colombia as missionaries. After being continents away from each other, we had years to catch up on and love to renew when we met again in the summer of 1985.

Linda's life is remarkable in itself with all the paths she has chosen—many of which would be too difficult for a weaker saint. Jim and Linda returned to South Africa in 1998 after pioneering a church in Orlando. Jim had a stroke, followed by the removal of an invasive brain tumor, two toe amputations from diabetes, a daughter on the run...well, you can see the call and perseverance they have had in serving the Lord.

Linda is refined gold. And after you read the letter she sent me, you will see that God uses everything the devil plans for evil in a Christian's life—even before we are saved. God gladly uses our mistakes, our bruises, our shattered earthen vessels that He alone is able to patch and polish into precious, glistening joy. I didn't know this secret about Linda before now, so how much more I appreciate her candor in sharing such a personal story.

Can I Forgive Myself?

"I wanted to write about my experiences on how valuable life is and about the ignorant, willful taking of it. This is hard, but I just couldn't let it go untold. Maybe someone else is in this position, and they should know that Abba Father has a big lap to crawl onto and sob, and on which to heal.

"Sitting here in South Africa twelve thousand miles away from the scene and twenty-eight after the fact, I feel removed from the horrible pain and guilt I experienced so many years ago. After I received Jesus, I asked the Lord, 'Why did I have to go through those ten years of deception and degradation? I came when You called me, Lord. Why didn't You call me before all that terrible stuff happened?'

"When the Lord did call me at the age of twenty-eight, I had participated in almost every conceivable sin the human mind can imagine. I was acting in movies, married, and twice divorced. I had...aborted two children. The first abortion was especially hideous, as it was in the illegal days. All the horror stories are real! By the time of the second abortion, it was legal, and my conscience was so seared. I was back partying after the third day.

If we confess our sins, He is faithful and just and will forgive us our sins and purify us from all unrighteousness. (1 John 1:9)

"But soon after the second abortion, Jesus came and found me. I was so pleased to find peace for my soul for all the sins I had committed, but when [Christians] said abortion was an act of murder, I just couldn't find forgiveness for myself for that! They kept telling me, 'But, Jesus has forgiven you. Who are you to not forgive yourself?'

"One night I dreamed of my two children I had aborted. One was a boy, the other was a girl. They were in heaven surrounded by angels. I seemed to understand that one day I would see them again, and they would know me and I would know them. It took me five years, but I finally forgave myself. I also understood why Jesus let me go through those years in sin, because I became very merciful to the sinner, as I had been one myself who desperately needed mercy."

God is so faithful, so good. Won't you who are in this same position as I was forgive yourself today and everyone else involved in the murder of your child? Let yourself be healed and become a lighthouse for others when it is time.

God will forgive you, if you will only ask Him and keep believing!

—Linda McCollum

Chapter 2

Abortion and Genetics

Christianity, in Jesus' time, was on the breaking edge of the cultural revolution. History has proven, with a few exceptions, that since then we Christians have lagged behind the times.

Will this continue in our current era of advances in science, medical research, and technological engineering? To reverse this trend, we need to connect the Word of God and His will with how we should act in faith in these areas. It's time to familiarize your theological positions with the new medical ethics sweeping the world at the speed of cybersonics.

This section will reveal the level of awareness we must have in order to get our theological wings flying. We begin with a group heralding the genocide happening all around us—the destruction of human life through abortion.

Are you ready to begin?

"Unusual" Circumstances

Lois and Greg Cunningham work with the Genocide Awareness Project at the University of Central Florida. As you may expect, they hear lots of questions and comments challenging their opposition to abortion. Here are answers to some of the questions kids generally ask about the validity of abortion in unusual circumstances. The answers were offered by the Michigan chapter of Right to Life and were sent to me by the Cunninghams.

What about pregnancy resulting from rape or incest?

While pregnancies from rape and incest are rare, the problems of the victims are serious indeed. But even if pregnancy results from such circumstances, two important considerations remain. First, abortion is not the cure-all for those women. In fact, abortion may increase the problems faced by many victims of rape or incest.

Secondly, the unfortunate circumstances of conception won't change the nature of the unborn child. We don't execute rapists or incestuous males, so why should we accept the execution of their innocent offspring?

One physician, Dr. Sandra Mahkorn, a former rape counselor in Chicago, found in her research on pregnancy resulting from rape that, far from solving the problems of pregnant rape victims, abortion for many women increased unhealthy feelings of denial, misplaced anger, and alienation.

In an analysis of incestuous pregnancies, Dr. George Maloof, a San Francisco psychiatrist, found that abortion was frequently encouraged—even forced, on occasion—by fathers who wished to conceal and continue an incestuous relationship with a now-pregnant daughter. Maloof also noted that, because of the unique nature of incest, abortion may serve to keep a young girl trapped in an incestuous relationship by removing her only tangible proof of its existence.

What is needed are practical, supportive, and effective assistance systems that benefit mother and child, whose lives have both been touched by violence. The violence of abortion solves little, if anything.

What about aborting disabled fetuses?

The notion that people are better off dead than disabled is an odd one, particularly in light of studies that indicate disabled persons commit suicide far less often than "normal" persons. Another study found that children severely damaged by the drug Thalidomide in the 1950s do indeed feel their lives are worthwhile and happy.

Imposing our own standards of perfection (physical and/or intellectual) in a lethal fashion onto the disabled presumes we can judge the value of their lives, surely the crassest kind of elitism.

Does abortion reduce child abuse?

In the professional literature, one would be hard-pressed to find even one reputable study that indicates unrestricted abortion reduces child abuse. In fact, according to a study by psychiatrist Dr. Philip Ney, increased abortion rates may actually contribute to rising rates of child abuse, principally by removing taboos on violence against children and interfering with important maternal-infant bonding processes.

A study by Dr. Edward Lenoski of the University of Southern California revealed that in one large sampling of child abuse cases, 90 percent involved children who were "planned" pregnancies. In his book *Somewhere a Child Is Crying*, Dr. Vincent J. Fontana, former chairman of the mayor's task force on child abuse and neglect of the city of New York, rejects abortion as a cure-all for child abuse.

Fontana notes, "It might be a wonderfully neat solution, if it were only valid...The assumption that every child is an unwanted child, or that most or even a large proportion of abused children are unwanted children, is totally false."

People should only have wanted children, right?

What does it mean to be "unwanted?" In this context, if someone doesn't want you, or if you aren't useful or pretty or convenient, you can be killed via abortion. It's important to remember that "unwantedness" doesn't magically disappear at birth, particularly when getting rid of the unwanted child after birth is looking so attractive to many professionals.

Consider "unwantedness" in the light of the waiting list of adoptive parents in this country. In Michigan, according to one adoption worker in the state Department of Social Services, to adopt a child under five years of age, a couple must wait an average of five years.

For harder-to-place disabled children there are existing medical and support subsidies to facilitate their adoption. Clearly, an "unwanted" child, even the classically hard-to-place child, is wanted by countless parents who can provide loving, caring homes. Why choose to kill when we can give the gift of life to *both* child and adoptive families?

Who is more vulnerable than the unborn? They have no clothes, no money, no property, no power. They cannot speak or organize to defend themselves. If their right to life is not recognized and protected, then they are completely vulnerable to power and violence and death.

—*Right to Life of Michigan*

A Bloody War

Like many in the life issues movement, Margaret J. Kinney sees the abortion struggle as all-out war. Here, she equates the pre-born with the slaves whose captivity tarnished our nation's history:

> "Our forefathers won the bloody Revolutionary War and gained the right to live free from oppression and tyranny of others—or so they thought. Eventually, Americans recognized the practice of slavery as the stealing of the slaves' God-given rights to pursue their own lives. Former President Ronald Reagan recalled Lincoln's response to slavery:

> *Abraham Lincoln recognized that we could not survive as a free land when some men could decide that others were not fit to be free and should therefore be slaves. The fate of slavery hung in the balance of the Civil War. Eventually, our brothers won the bloody Civil War and gained freedom from enslavement to the wills of others, or so they thought.*
>
> *Many years later, a remnant of Americans began to recognize the practice of abortion as the stealing of unborn babies' God-given rights to life...Likewise, we cannot survive as a free nation when some men decide that others are not fit to live and should be abandoned to abortion or infanticide.*
>
> *My administration is dedicated to the preservation of America as a free land, and there is no cause more important for preserving that freedom than affirming the transcendent right to life of all human beings, the right without which no other rights have any meaning.*

"Millions of unborn babies have been aborted in our lifetime. Where is their right to live free from oppression and the tyranny of others? Where is their freedom from enslavement to the will of others? Yes, we have won some important battles for the right to life, but the war still rages on. This time the blood is being spilt in the wombs of mothers around the world.

"The fate of future unborn generations rests within our hands. How will history judge us? Will we win the bloody war on abortion? Human life is a direct gift of God. To violate that gift is to violate God, a just God whose 'justice cannot sleep forever." We must rise to meet the challenge, because the most important question is not 'How will history judge us?' but 'How will God judge us?' "

—*Margaret J. Kinney*

Life and Justice

It's worthwhile at this point to quote Dónal P. O'Mathúna, from his contribution, *Applying Justice to Genetics,* because he takes us logically to the next step on the slippery slope of denying inalienable rights to certain humans.

As O'Mathúna understands, you cannot separate life and justice in God's universe any more than you can separate wetness from water. When one is compromised, both are compromised. O'Mathúna states it this way:

"To truly practice justice incorporates a refusal to shed innocent blood. Justice demands that all people be comforted and nourished. According to the Bible, all people are images of God and thus should be treated with the same level of respect. Yet genetic essentialism categorizes people into those deserving of full respect and those deserving little or no respect.

"Some of the unborn are viewed as so genetically disadvantaged that their parents owe it to society not to bring them to term. These infants must be sacrificed on the altar of society's prosperity and the family's lifestyle. Some material things have become more important than life itself.

"Sometimes concern about the unnecessary suffering of a disabled child is really concern for the suffering this child might cause those around the child. These decisions reflect the assumption that some lives are not worth living.

"Genetic testing is thereby used to determine whether the unborn meet the genetic qualifications required to merit life. Genetic testing used for this purpose violates biblical justice. Healing in the Bible involves restoring people to health. They were not being made taller, faster, or more beautiful.

"In fact, the Hebrew term for healing means to restore something to its original condition, or make it whole again. This implies that something intrinsically wrong or dysfunctional was being corrected. Thus, overcoming the groaning and suffering of this present age is one way people can be faithful images of God."

Medicine in general, and genetic technology in particular, should be used to prevent or relieve suffering and disease. However, only those traits that are inherently dysfunctional or cause pain and suffering should be treated. Having a trait that falls outside normalcy or that is not valued by society does not justify its medical manipulation. In other words, genetic therapy should treat only consequences of the Fall, not the results of genetic diversity.

The Value of One Life: Joni Eareckson Tada

It was before seven o'clock in the morning when I curled up with Joni's lovely illustrated book, knowing that all those little lines in her artwork were carefully placed there by a pencil in her mouth. Joni broke her back in a diving accident more than thirty years ago and now uses the only non-paralyzed parts of her body—from her shoulders up—to glorify God.

In the middle of Joni's volume came the touching story of Cody. He serves as the perfect example of the sanctity of life, a life others would throw away.

Joni explained that Cody had been born with the umbilical cord wrapped around his neck, leaving him paralyzed and unable to speak. He was deaf and blind. He needed a ventilator in order to breathe and a feeding tube in order to eat—a lot of baggage for a seventeen-month-old baby in foster care.

He did respond when someone caressed his cheeks and, although Joni could not feel that sweet little cheek because of her own disabilities, Cody could. Here, let Joni tell her story:

> "...(A)s I stroked him, I thought I saw a faint smile. I prayed silently, asking God to be large in Cody's heart, to comfort and console him, to speak 'not in words taught us by human wisdom but in words taught by the Spirit' (1 Corinthians 2:13).
>
> "I thought of those who would say, 'Take out his feeding tube. Let him starve to death. His life has no meaning, no purpose.' But 2 Corinthians 5:16 warns us to 'regard no one from a worldly point of view.'
>
> "Elsewhere, we are reminded that 'inwardly we are being renewed day by day. For our light and momentary troubles are achieving for us an eternal glory that far outweighs them all. So we fix our eyes not on what is seen, but on what is unseen' (2 Corinthians 4:16-18).
>
> "God's Word is as true for Cody as it is for anyone. The Spirit expresses truth to him—not in audible words, but in spiritual words. Inwardly he is being renewed. His troubles are achieving for him an eternal glory. His value is 'not on what is seen, but on what is unseen.' Therefore, we are not to regard him from a worldly point of view.

"The Spirit is dynamic, active, and powerful, and although we can't see the spiritual activity happening in Cody's life, it's there. His is a hidden holiness. We can't measure God's work or quantify it—but it's real. And spiritual activity gives life value, no matter how humble a person's situation. Cody isn't doing much more than living and being.

"But God has His reasons. Ours is an intentional God, brimming over with motive and mission. He never does things capriciously or decides with the flip of a coin. And His design for that little boy is to simply live, breathe, and encourage others. It's enough to give life meaning and purpose."

—Joni Eareckson Tada

Vigil on the War Front

One crisp autumn day while walking in front of an abortuary in Orlando, I began a vigil of prayer since I was not experienced in sidewalk referral counseling. It was scary, but back and forth I went, holding a Bible opened to Isaiah and the Psalms, where God said He would vindicate the needy. I prayed the Bible verses out loud, arm raised to heaven...pacing as car horns honked their rebuke. My thoughts turned to the womb. What kind of place was that? Why did we all love it there so much? What of the babies inside this building, not thirty feet away, being pulled loose, the shock of cold air, the blood and violence, the unsummoned trip back to Father? Such a short time on Earth.

As I was gazing over the rooftop into the sky, I suddenly had a vision of teardrop shapes rising toward heaven—wispy, wrapped in swaddles of prayer—and I asked God as unbidden tears streamed down my cheeks, "Why did You show this to me? I've never had an abortion. Never came close. We adopted two children others threw away. Why am *I* crying for these infants who are not even mine?"

And the Lord told me very gently, "Those are My children. I am crying for them. You are privileged to weep My tears for them; they are aware of that. You need to feel the injustice of it, the pain of it, the heartbreak of it all; feel the abject insult to the Giver of life when My gifts are flung back with such violent ingratitude. Your presence here is to have your prayers and love escort them back to Me, the Giver of all life. They know."

It broke my heart and changed me forever. That day, I never spoke a word to the mothers, the doctor or nurses, the guard at the door, the accomplices who swaggered by with their pitiful, macho attitudes. These men do not know that a real man cares for his lady and protects his children from danger until well into their own adulthood.

No, all that went unspoken. But I thought of the womb and what God had perfectly fashioned—what His exact will was for all those allowed to stay for the full nine months.

The human womb is a marvelous place. It is warm and dark, velvety soft and pulsing with life—the perfect hideout for the most vulnerable period of our development. Sounds filter in with sleepy rhythms that rock us, as budding limbs and feet, hands and delicate organs hourly flourish into unique beauty. It is peaceful there, and safe.

God's magnificent method of forming us in the womb cannot be improved. Isaiah quotes the very words of God, who explains to future generations that He is the Redeemer, the originator of human life. He compares the complexity of our formation to His work of creating all things from the subatomic to the grand cosmic. The womb is a world as much as the heavens and the earth, and He gives it special significance and respect.

"This is what the Lord says—Your Redeemer, who formed you in the womb: I am the Lord, who has made all things, who alone stretched out the heavens, who spread out the earth by myself." (Isaiah 44:24)

---

* * * * *

Can you imagine the Trinity in a creative mood?

Stretching out the vast expanse of the heavens, placing each star—by name—where it will be a constant wonder until its assignment is over? Billions of galaxies, innumerable stars, planets, blazing suns, fresh novas, reflecting moons—but only one Earth He spread out, "by Myself."

If you falter in times of trouble, how small is your strength! Rescue those being led away to death; hold back those staggering toward slaughter. If you say, 'But we knew nothing about this,' does not He who weighs the heart perceive it? Does not He who guards your life know it? Will He not repay each person according to what He has done? (Proverbs 24:10-12)

Then, with the utmost complexity, He deposited the human ovum where it could be joined by the marvelously energetic sperm making that first cell, able to proliferate into wholeness according to its divine DNA encoding. God provided those rapidly doubling cells with the warm darkness of nourishment and love and called it the womb.

If you are distressed today and want to crawl back into bed, curl up, and pull the covers over your head, it may be that your inner spirit is longing to enter a place of safety and serenity. You just need time to regroup, center your soul, and know the Lord Jesus more deeply in this particular circumstance.

And remember that the womb is for developing babies. How very much we older kids need our heavenly Father when we are weary from the battles of life.

Next we go to other nations to see how they battle for life.

Chapter 3

Life Awareness in Other Nations

Having close ties with the European life-issues movement based in Holland, I have learned that the Dutch are a fiercely patriotic and freedom-loving people. Two of those people are Drs. Bert Dorenbos and his wife, Willy, who organize conferences, usually held in November, for leaders in more than thirty nations as far away as South Africa, where a very strong medical organization works for life.

For years, Drs. Dorenbos was the CEO of television and radio media in Holland but left to join Willy in the life issues effort after seeing *The Scream for Life* film the first time. It rocked his world and brought to the forefront of the European life issues movement one of the strongest life heroes of our generation.

The War in the Womb

Here are Drs. Dorenbos' thoughts on what abortion has wrought in the nations of the world:

"Mother Teresa left her influential position as a well-trained nun to step down and identify herself with the poorest of the poor. She gave them a cup of water before they died in the streets of India. After receiving the peace prize money from the explosion specialist Alfred Nobel in Copenhagen, she exclaimed that the world was suffering from the Third World War raging in the mothers' wombs. This is a war in which more than fifty million victims are taken every year—as much as the carnage of the whole Second World War.

"After more than fifty years, more than one-half billion children have been aborted by their mothers. The suffering goes on in one way or the other with post-abortion syndrome. [Abortion] is declaring war on humankind. It is a gigantic opening for the demons to have permission to continue to kill and destroy, one little baby at a time. The world listened to this tiny nun from Calcutta but went on with their war in the mother's womb anyway.

"Killing another human being to solve your problem is never the solution to your problem.

"It was the cynical Malcolm Muggeridge of the BBC-UK who saw this little woman in his travels in Calcutta and was so impressed that he wrote *Something Beautiful for God,* making her a world-renowned figure. Muggeridge started looking for truth after his encounter with Mother Teresa. We met him several times and talked a lot until he wrote his last book, *From Dust to Destiny,* which followed on the heels of *Chronicles of Wasted Time.*

"These books came forth because he understood that truth and reality were only found in the eternal truth of the revelation of God. It took all his life to find out this truth, and his journey of life [presents] a call for everyone else to make the shortcut and accept the truth of the heavenly revelation. This is how you can truly find peace for yourself and declare peace for the world.

"To allow and foster abortion means a society has declared war on itself. In this sense, it is 'civil war,' meaning that the citizens themselves are against each other—killing each other—not against outside enemies as in regular warfare. "

—Drs. Bert Dorenbos

Civil War

Abortion *is* civil war! It decimates a nation from within. And its population can get so low that it will become too weak to fight off real enemies should they come to take the land.

It's obvious that declaring war on unborn babies is the utmost cruelty mankind can devise. In ancient history, only pagan peoples killed their own children, and then it was to appease demonic gods. We can only hope that the time will come when civilized people will conclude they cannot accept abortion as a solution to *any* problem.

Social inequities were banished once before, as godly activists fought against slavery. But how then is it possible that six million Jews (and other "undesirables") could be declared lower than flies and animals, a waste to society, and then killed? That should make us think.

It's clear that although we have a sophisticated intelligence, we can still come up with disastrous "solutions" like killing off those who do not fit into the current thinking about what is acceptable.

The danger that any group could be the target of discrimination is very close, at any time and at any place. We have to be alert to the threat that we could be heading toward a new discriminative arena. Remember, when legalized abortion was on the horizon, nobody ever thought euthanasia would be next.

Those who warned about the potential threat of euthanasia were called crazy or right-wing fundamentalists. But euthanasia did arrive on the scene, and some people found it to be a very logical way of handling difficult situations. Abortion, the killing of an unborn human being, and euthanasia, the killing of a born human being, are identical. There is no difference in principle.

Theology of Euthanasia

We have to go deeper in our understanding of the reasons why modern man justifies euthanasia. A theology on euthanasia is important to develop, because life issues people need to be clear on their own positions. Assuredly, life is precious in the sight of the Lord. He gives life and He takes life.

Death was a result of sin in Eden. Death will change at the moment Jesus comes back and we enter His eternal kingdom of right and righteousness.

That much we are sure of.

Secularists think euthanasia is a way to get rid of suffering. Suffering is seen as a negative aspect of living, and the sooner it is gotten rid of, the better. They say, "Life should be without pain and suffering. Every suffering we can prevent will be good for society" and "We are happy to see that modern medical knowledge is able to cure and prevent a lot of suffering."

But suffering is part of what it means to be human, part of the burden placed on us when Adam sinned against God. Suffering does have meaning in life. Suffering often brings a person to terms with himself and with God.

Few people can imagine the blessings that can come from suffering, but they do come. This is true not only for the patient, but also for those around him or her. By killing a person to alleviate pain and suffering, we cut off any possibility that he or she will come to understand the eternal consequences of suffering. Suffering is a natural mechanism designed to bring a person to repent and accept the Lord before his or her death, when there are no more chances.

Euthanasia denies reality. It seeks a utopian world without pain and suffering. And taking the concept to its logical conclusion, weak human beings run the risk of becoming unwilling victims of euthanasia practices, especially when those practices include eliminating the lives of those whose "quality of life" is diminished.

Euthanasia has opened the door for an active killing mentality where only those who contribute to society have the right of life. This total change of direction is dangerous for mankind. Instead of caring for those in need, society is heading in the direction of getting rid of those who require extra care, time, and community resources.

Some people are born disabled, others become disabled; some will suffer a lot as they age, while some will die instantly at a young or old age. We know for sure that everyone will die.

But that is *not* the same as being a victim.

* * * * *

In Holland the discussion about what to do with the terminally ill in the last hours of life started in the 1970s. The Dutch wanted to establish a method to help doctors determine when they could stop providing treatment when there was no good prognosis. It was from these concerns that the discussion of euthanasia started.

More than twenty years later, the Dutch have reached a place where, in principle, everyone has the right to decide when it is time to die, without penalizing the doctor who assists.

The first case approved by the courts was that of a woman in her fifties who was physically healthy but depressed because her husband had died. She requested that a doctor come to kill her, which he did.

The court decided that the doctor made the right decision—except he did not consult a fellow doctor, which was a necessary step according to legal protocol. Then, a new proposal was passed that exempted doctors who practiced euthanasia from criminal prosecution.

This isn't the first time in modern history that this has happened, of course, because in Nazi Germany, Hitler gave German doctors permission to kill patients who were terminally ill. Thousands upon thousands of the elderly, demented, and disabled children and adults were legally killed. The first gas chambers in history were built for these patients.

Murder is murder. There are no exceptions. By accepting exclusions, the Dutch have turned an objective rule into a subjective measure. All we have to do is wait to see which is the next category of people who will be excluded from criminal punishment under the penal code, because that will happen.

The length and breadth of abuse is now wide open in Holland. Lawyers and courts around the world need to protest and shame Holland into reversing this deadly decision.

The Legality of Euthanasia

From a legal point of view, euthanasia must never be acceptable. The powerful euthanasia lobby is fighting, not so much for the terminally ill, but for your right to decide to kill yourself at the moment you would like to die, the moment when you want to step out of society.

This has always been an issue. Throughout history, people have wanted to kill themselves on their own terms for many reasons. But up until now, a potential victim of suicide has always been seen as a person who needed to be rescued from self-harm.

"For every living soul belongs to me, the father as well as the son—both alike belong to me." (Ezekiel 18:4)

The Dutch law gives the individual the right to kill himself and request help in the process! The law pointedly ignores the natural law that life does not belong to a person. Life has been given, and it will be required back by the One to whom it belongs; nobody knows when or how. Taking your own life is against the natural development of being human.

Caring or Mercy Killing?

It's amazing that in these days of greatly developed medical skills and knowledge the medical profession cannot come up with better solutions than to kill its patients—because with the application of care and compassion, the question of euthanasia as a last resort simply fades away. The hospice movement in Britain provides proof that wherever the hospice system is used to care for the terminally ill, there is no call for euthanasia.

Doctors and nurses should be the very last to accept euthanasia. They never should be willing or forced to take an active role in practicing euthanasia at another's request, especially since they have pledged to use their skills for curing their patients and not for killing them. And a doctor should know the precise moment when his curing capability is futile and turn the patient over to the caring hands of those who help people die naturally and without pain.

Compassionate people understand that pain can be a severe part of suffering. But in this age of palliative knowledge and care, we never should accept euthanasia as an alternative. And where pain reduction has not been developed to the modern level of treatment, it should be implemented as quickly as possible.

In the United States, about 40 percent of all hospice care facilities are operated by religious organizations. This is an area that cries out for volunteer help from the local church, enabling patients to receive not only physical help but spiritual assistance as well.

Introducing legal killing into society in order to solve a problem can never be a solution. Doing so presents a clear danger to all members of society, because one day, each of us may face such a situation, and we will be powerless to follow our God in His methods of natural death.

Israel for Life

Finally, we have this report from Israel:

"In Israel, there are about eighteen thousand surgical abortions per year approved by health ministry-appointed committees. In addition, according to the former health minister, Shoshanna Arbeli-Almozlino, two illegal abortions are performed for every legal one.

"Since the establishment of the nation, it is estimated that there have been more than one million surgical abortions performed. Free abortions are available for teenagers and soldiers.

"According to the Israeli women's magazine, *La Isha,* late-term abortions are performed after twenty-three weeks of gestation at twelve hospitals.

"The Knesset (Israel's parliament) legalized abortion in 1977, after abortion was made legal in the United Kingdom and the United States. By law, a pregnant woman can 'interrupt her pregnancy' at a recognized medical institution.

"Abortion is permitted if:

(1) the woman is under 18 years old or over 40

(2) the pregnancy was due to relations prohibited by criminal law—incest, rape, adultery, or premarital sex

(3) the unborn child has any physical or mental defect

(4) continuation of the pregnancy is likely to endanger the woman's life or cause her physical or emotional harm

"Only the Lord knows the number of unborn babies that die as a result of using chemical birth control products, such as the intrauterine Device (IUD), Norplant, RU-486, Depo-Provera, the morning after pill, the mini-pill, and The Pill...all of these birth control methods either sometimes or often alter the mother's womb in a way that causes it to reject the human life that God designed it to nourish and sustain. The IUD is widely used by religious women who have not been told these facts by their physicians or rabbis."

—Ted Walker, national director of Be'ad Chaim

* * * * *

These first three chapters have provided an overview of different settings for decision's on life and death matters. The following chapter ends our section on the sanctity of life, with personal stories and appeals to compassion to balance out legal and science matters.

We have made rules and legalized them into punishable bits and pieces. When you break the law (even if you do not know what it is), fines and/or jail terms are imposed. There are so many rules and laws in all cultures that it would be impossible to keep them updated and published on a regular basis.

In this regard, Jesus Christ offered a breath of fresh air. He came to break the power of the law of Moses to the extent that we are forced to think twice, forgive without impunity, and show compassion to all. That is much more difficult than keeping rules.

Chapter 4

Compassion and Science

There is no doubt about it: The defense of life is an emotionally charged subject. People feel strongly about it and are willing to put those feelings into terse electronic messages to inform and encourage the more timid to formulate their own opinions and, hopefully, to act on them in a very positive way for the best of society.

Sometimes this takes the form of a letter to the editor.

Truth or Consequences?

Life issues activist Patte Smith sent the following letter to her local newspaper, expressing her thoughts on the subject of the man who caused a car crash that killed the pre-born twins of the pregnant driver of the other car.

> "Kenneth Michael Hinson runs a red light in Lake Mary and kills two 27-week-old fetuses.

> Consequence: Hinson is arrested for vehicular homicide. Abortionist James Scott Pendergraft, M.D., kills 27-week-old fetuses (and older) for two years in Orlando. Consequence: Pendergraft receives more than two thousand dollars per fetus as payment. It's a tragic injustice that some people are punished while others are rewarded for feticide in Central Florida."

Hinson, whose license had been suspended or revoked ten times for driving under the influence, ran a red light and crashed his truck into a car driven by the pregnant woman. She was carrying her first babies—twins, both of whom died. It turns out that Hinson had had his *automobile* driving privileges revoked, but not his *truck* driving privileges.

When unborn babies accidentally die as a result of another's malfeasance or negligence, it is prosecuted as a homicide. Why then do we have a double standard by allowing intentional, paid-for murders of pre-borns by calling them abortions?

Does this make *any* sense? Furthermore, a fetus killed in an auto crash is positively identified as the loss of a fully human person, not just the loss of a blob of tissue.

Giving Up Your Life

Standing up for life sometimes means giving up your life. This depth of living is far more costly than the loss of physical existence, since we all face eternal rewards and consequences.

Giving your life might mean serving jail time for righteousness, long periods of time away from your family, suffering injustice, or being fined millions of dollars all because you stood and prayed near an abortion clinic.

It means being active in kingdom work, whatever the consequences to your physical life. Generations of missionaries know all about that.

Will you ever be asked to lay down your life? Or lay down your life for another—perhaps for a stranger, a tiny fetus, the weak, those being "led away to death" as the Bible says. It can happen out of the blue, in the blink of an eye, at the behest of an assailant or a tyrant. Christians do give their lives.

"So long as parents are willing to place their careers and goals ahead of the very lives of their children, the world will become an increasingly hostile and sad place in which to live." —Douglas R. Scott, president, Life Decisions International

---

Dietrich Bonhoeffer was right when he said, "It is before that Cross and not before us that the world trembles." We must hold the Cross high as a beacon so that the world may tremble.

Shouting at Evil

Two front-line soldiers in the fight against abortion are Terri and Tim Palmquist. Here, they issue a caution against some of the more militant means of fighting the battles and urge pro-lifers to focus on extending mercy to those who need it most.

> "The culture war is over. The battle is lost. Or so 'they' say. Our society, our culture has fallen into the hands of robbers. Children in America today don't know what it is to have one set of parents that remain married to one another 'until death do us part.'
>
> "They don't know what it is to go to school without fear. They don't know there is a right and a wrong; that truth is not subjective, that all life is valuable.
>
> "We in the Christian community have gone from moral outrage to righteous indignation and finally, to defeat. We feel we've lost. We no longer maintain the moral majority. We have picketed and paraded. We have voted. We have prayed. We have shouted at evil with all we are, only to end in resignation and despair."

"'Which of these three do you think was a neighbor to the man who fell into the hands of robbers?' The expert in the law replied, 'The one who had mercy on him.' Jesus to him, 'Go and do likewise.'" (Luke 10:36-37)

> "But what did Jesus tell us to do? 'Go and do likewise.' Like the Good Samaritan who had

mercy on his neighbor who fell victim to thieves, we are to have mercy, to show love to those in our spheres of influence who have fallen victim to Satan's ploys.

"We cannot defeat evil by shouting at it. We cannot cause it to retreat by our outrage and indignation, deserved though it may be. The truth lies not in what we shout from our rooftops, but by how we live in the quietness of our homes and in the streets of our communities.

"'Love your enemies. Pray for those who persecute you.' These words of instruction have left us. Not 'Beat people up with your picket signs' or 'Torch the local abortuary.'

"Shouting at evil only serves to fuel evil. Being evil, it fuels more evil.

"Instead, try whispering some love to an enemy today. Nothing disarms an enemy like an act of mercy. See if it doesn't make a difference in our world, one person at a time."

—Terri and Tim Palmquist,
Bakersfield, California

That brand of mercy is what the Palmquists had to practice with a young woman who was recently helped through their LifeSavers Ministries. Her name has been changed at her request, but her story is typical of the way Terri and Tim have ministered to pregnant women—and their boyfriends, husbands, and families—over the past sixteen years. Here is

"Lucinda's" account of her contact with this special couple.

Lucinda's Story

"In August of last year, I went to a hotel for two days to contemplate my decision on having an abortion. I was thirteen weeks pregnant. Even though I knew it was wrong, I made an appointment and kept trying to convince myself by thinking, 'I'm not that far along for it to even be a baby yet. It probably isn't even formed. What's the big deal?'

"My life was a disaster. My husband didn't care about me or the pregnancy (even though he wanted to start a family—now that I was pregnant, he said he's not ready to be a father). He couldn't provide a place for us to live. He was living with his parents, but I couldn't live there because his mom despises me.

"My family disowned me because I chose to marry my husband. They stopped talking to me once they knew I was pregnant. I remember my sister telling me, 'Oh great. That's all the world needs is another Rick. If you have this kid the family won't be too happy with you.'

"I couldn't take it anymore. I had no husband, no family, and no job—all because I was pregnant.

"On the night before my scheduled abortion, I tried to sleep but couldn't. My thoughts were so twisted. I tried so hard to justify what I was going to do that I even prayed for God to help me and for Him to know that I wasn't doing this because I wanted to, but because I had to.

"I didn't want to have a baby with my husband if we weren't going to be together. If I had the abortion, my problems would be solved. My family wouldn't be upset with me, and I would be able to go back to work.

"At around 10:45 that night, I turned on the radio, trying to get my mind off the abortion. When I began fumbling through the stations, I paused for a while to listen to a talk show. But it wasn't a talk show—it was a Christian broadcaster talking about abortion! He began mentioning how abortion was a sin and how God hurts when the life of one of His innocent creations is taken before they are even born. I quickly shut off the radio. I didn't want to hear anymore.

"The next morning I called the radio station. [They] called Terri Palmquist, and later that day, Terri brought me to LifeHouse where I talked and prayed with her and her husband, Tim. Terri thought Tim might be able to talk some sense into Rick, so Tim made contact and went for a drive with Rick. Rick told Tim he would get an apartment for us in a couple of weeks.

"I missed my abortion appointment, but I hadn't really changed my mind yet. Terri said I could stay at LifeHouse until Rick and I got an apartment. Over the next few weeks, Rick and I talked a lot.

"At times, it seemed that Rick might finally take responsibility for me and the baby. But when the time came to make a commitment to the landlord of an apartment, he would put me off again and again! His last promise was that he would have all his outstanding bills paid by the time the baby was born, and then he would find us a place to live so we could be a real family.

"LifeSavers was willing to let me stay at LifeHouse until the baby was born, but I was an emotional wreck. At the time when I really needed my family, I couldn't go to them because they wouldn't help unless I divorced Rick, which was very tempting. But I kept hoping that once he saw the baby, he would change.

"Several times over the next few weeks, thoughts of having an abortion would pop into my head, but there was always a 'LifeSaver' around to talk to."

If anyone does not provide for his relatives, and especially for his immediate family, he has denied the faith and is worse than an unbeliever. (Timothy 5:8)

> "Then, on January 20, Ricardo M. III was born! What a sweet blessing he is! As for his father, he still refuses to be a husband and father. Little Ricky and I are still staying at LifeHouse.
>
> If it wasn't for LifeSavers, my baby wouldn't be here and I might not be here either. To Tim and Terri Palmquist, and all of you who helped to keep *LifeHouse* open over the last six months, my baby and I will always be thankful. May God bless you for all you've done."
>
> *—Lucinda*

Compassion: David Reardon

David Reardon is the author of an important book, *Making Abortion Rare: A Healing Strategy for a Divided Nation.* He encourages Christians—especially those whose loved ones have had abortions—to keep a scripture from Matthew 6 ever in their minds and hearts: "If you do not forgive others, neither will your Father forgive you." He believes Christians must heed that verse in this abortion battle within the war for life.

> "How do you react if a loved one confesses to having been involved in a past abortion? What if it was your spouse? Or your mother? A brother or sister? Your best friend? Would you rebuke them with a condemning, angry, or disappointed attitude?
>
> "Or would you instantly embrace them to show your willingness to share their sorrow

and regrets? Could you listen with patience and love, even if they were still trying to defend what they had done?

"These are important questions. The decision you make today to be understanding, compassionate, and forgiving can shape your emotions and reactions in the future. Will you be a hindrance to post-abortion healing or an ambassador of Christ's healing mercy?

"Millions of women, men, grandparents, children, and siblings are carrying about with them the pain of past abortions. These people are all around you. But many have never shared their secret with you because they are afraid of rejection. They doubt the mercy of both God and Christ's body, the church.

"To promote healing, we need to wear our compassion on our sleeves. Through our understanding, we can help to lift others from the sorrow of shame to the joy of hope.

"Pray today that you will not let your own pride or self-righteousness create an obstacle to the healing and reconciliation of your loved ones. Look for opportunities to tell others that your heart goes out to those who have lost a child to abortion. In this way, you will let others know that you are approachable.

"If you struggle with forgiving others, meditate on the Lord's Prayer. Every time we pray 'Forgive us our trespasses, as we forgive those who trespass against us,' we are entering into a covenant with God.

"We will be judged either liberally or stringently according to our own way of dealing with others. If we hold resentments against others, God will judge us using the same harsh measure. If we forgive others freely, God will forgive us freely.

"I am not saying that forgiveness is always easy. But I am saying that forgiveness is always possible and always necessary. Turn to God in prayer and ask for His help in forgiving others and in developing a forgiving attitude. Look to the example of Christ on the cross. Even in the midst of His agony, He cried out words of understanding and forgiveness—'Father, forgive them, for they know not what they do.'

"So, too, Christians must learn how to forgive even while we are still hurting. To do so, we must strive to see with the eyes of Christ, knowing that far more often than not, they know not what they are doing.'

We all make bad decisions for all kinds of reasons. Forgive them—not because our failures don't matter—but because they matter so much that we need each other to recover from the pain caused by our own mistakes.

—David Reardon

* * * * *

For the next four chapters, we will turn to the science of "Life for Sale." Yes, life is for sale, whether due to research goals, the lust for power in discovering the perfect gene sequence, or owning patents on humans for profit. Believe it or not, "religious" reasons also crop up and sometimes sound so right that we become confused about what God's opinion is.

Having choices in life is what life is all about. But our task as believers in the Lord Jesus Christ is to discover His will and please Him in the choices we make. That will often cross both our will and the culture's solutions to identical situations.

In these new technological areas, we must form a biblical basis for righteous living. And it's possible to do that, or God wouldn't ask us to.

Please pray as you read on, aware that new thinking might be ahead and that you may be crossing uncharted waters.

Section II

Biogenetic Realities

Chapter 5

Life for Sale

Dr. Stephen Hawking, mathematician, cosmologist, and astrophysicist, is indisputably the most brilliant man alive today, surpassing the venerable Albert Einstein. He is wheelchair-bound and paralyzed except for one finger. He needs and gets total care. A computer now expresses his thoughts, for up to an hour a day when he is physically up to it.

Is there enough "quality of life" to permit someone like Dr. Hawking to continued his existence? Can fetal tissue help him and, if so, should it be used? Is one diseased person's life of greater worth than that of an infant who cannot breathe on its own? Is it right to take that infant's life in order to provide body organs or tissues to the first person who needs them?

Which life do you judge to be more valuable—or are they equal?

"Suffering is a misfortune as viewed from the one side, and a discipline as viewed from the other." —Samuel Smiles

---

There are other philosophical questions that need answers. For example, since a person is going to be killed anyway (say, by abortion or capital crime punishment), doesn't it make perfect humanistic sense to use their body parts to help save the gravely ill?

Putting aside the emotionalism of desperate physical situations, we must look to the commercial side of these transactions. Is it proper for others—sometimes multiple layers of buyers, wholesalers, retailers, medical bureaucrats, doctors and technicians in the body parts business—to profit enormously from the pain, suffering, and death of the fetus or the condemned prisoner?

This is repugnant to those who adhere to the Old Morality. And don't even try to take money out of the equation, because this *is all about money*.

A Word From Pearl S. Buck

Pearl Buck, the famous author born in China of missionary parents, gave birth to a profoundly retarded daughter with PKU (phenylketonuria). She expressed her sentiments this way:

> "A retarded child, a handicapped person, brings its own gift to life, even to the life of normal human beings. That gift is comprehended in the lessons of patience,

> understanding, and mercy, which we all need to receive and to practice with one another. My feelings can be summed up, perhaps, by saying that in this world, where cruelty prevails in so many aspects of our life, I would not add the weight of choice to kill rather than to let live."

But this could be a sentimental parent speaking, someone who has probed the heart of God on the matter.

What if a profoundly retarded child was born into your family? Would you consider having another baby to harvest its parts to help save the first one—say, by the sharing of kidneys? When does the point come when one submits to the will of God and simply believes that sometimes He sends precious spirits and souls to indwell "inadequate" bodies?

Is the inconvenience of caring for an elderly relative with incurable dementia worth laying down your own life? Is their life as valuable as yours? Will you put your life on hold to raise an illegitimate grandchild, or will you do away with "the problem" through the death sentence of elective abortion?

Bible-believing Christians and Jews know that the human spirit, soul, and biological materials (body, organs, tissues, body parts) surmount some arbitrary market value placed upon them by secularists, no matter the age, viability, disabilities, criminal standing or racial characteristics of the person.

That means the decision to sell or donate organs, as well as to buy or receive human materials, makes the transaction a moral one. Prostituting oneself for any perceived gain, including altruism, violates the sanctity of God's gift of life. Humans are made in God's image. For this alone, they deserve respect and protection in every way.

The Word couples the immoral, unjustifiable taking of human life with the duty to procreate human life. There is a "not killing" command chained to the command to "be fruitful and multiply."

> "But you must not eat meat that has its lifeblood still in it. And for your lifeblood I will surely demand an accounting. I will demand an accounting from every animal. And from each man, too, I will demand an accounting for the life of his fellow man. Whoever sheds the blood of man, by man shall his blood be shed; for in the image of God has God made man. As for you, be fruitful and increase in number; multiply on the earth and increase upon it" (Genesis 9:4-7).
>
> "Any Israelite or any alien living among them who eats any blood—I will set my face against that person who eats blood and will cut him off from his people. For the life of a creature is in the blood, and I have given it to you to make atonement for yourselves on the altar; it is the blood that makes atonement for one's life. Therefore I say to the Israelites,
>
> "'None of you may eat blood, nor may an alien living among you eat blood.' Any Israelite or any alien living among you who

> hunts any animal or bird that may be eaten must drain out the blood and cover it with earth, because the life of every creature is its blood." (Leviticus 17:8-14)

This is where capital punishment gets its validation—a life for a life—and is the basis upon which some religious groups prohibit blood transfusions. Blood, unlike eyes, glands, hearts, kidneys, and other body components, is a renewable resource. The body can lose a certain amount of blood or plasma, and within time, the level will rise again to normal limits because blood is produced from within the body.

An extreme loss of blood can cause death. Blood carries health, as well as disease (like hepatitis) and viruses (such as HIV) that are incurable and final. There is so much we do not know about human blood, yet we do know its preservation is sacred to God and is to be respected as the gift of life.

Awash In Death

We are awash in death and the means by which it can be accomplished. What can turn us back toward a culture that accepted humbly from the hand of fate the fact that death came to everyone at its appointed time? The movement of the 1920s and 1930s for legalizing euthanasia had grown within secular and liberal religious circles and seemed to reach its zenith within the next 20 years.

Opinions in the 1950s showed a growing support for assisted suicide and euthanasia. No doubt people were tired of the bloodbath of World War II and sought a more gentle passing.

The ethics firmly planted by Carl F. H. Henry, a founding faculty member of Fuller Theological Seminary, German theologian Karl Barth, and Christian ethicist Paul Ramsey resisted these trends as Christians were given biblical guidelines and deeper understanding into God's character related to the sanctity of life.

"For every living soul belongs to me, the father as well as the son—both alike belong to me." (Ezekiel 18:4)

Human Genome Project

The goal of the massive Human Genome Project is to identify the entire human genetic blueprint. The genetic blueprint is known as a genome. Genes are inherited from the parental lines and sometimes contain potential problems.

For instance, diseases like Huntington's chorea, Alzheimer's, diabetes, breast cancer, Down syndrome, cystic fibrosis, birth defects, and Duchenne's dystrophy all stem from genetic factors.

Finding this out is not bad. It is what we do with this information—in racial, class, gender, viability, or health situations—that counts. In this instance, democracy may not be a friend but a foe, if the majority votes for the elimination of some citizens who have what is considered through the microscopic eyes of the biogeneticist to be "undesirable" genetic markers or potential problems.

If that proves true, must all the pre-born—for example with Down syndrome—be eliminated, regardless of the parents' willingness to keep their child?

Nuremberg Trials

Another mitigating factor was the filming of the Nuremberg trials in the late 1940s. That was when the world learned how Nazi Germany had applied the concepts of eugenics ("improving" the race), human experimentation, racism, euthanasia for imbeciles and those with "no quality of life," and the systematic annihilation of mentally ill inmates. The outcome of this in the years that followed was that some thirty-five American states outlawed assisted suicide and all fifty states classified euthanasia as murder.

A young law professor, Yale Kamisar, was appalled by a faction that pleaded for the right of rational persons who suffered from incurable, painful afflictions to choose death. In 1958, Kamisar wrote a landmark law-review article that set the parameters for subsequent legal debates about physician-assisted suicide and euthanasia law. Kamisar stated:

> "I am willing to accept civil liberties as the battlefield, but issues of 'liberty' and

> 'freedom' mean little until we begin to pin down *whose* liberty and freedom and for *what* need and at *what* price. I am more concerned about the life and liberty of those who would needlessly be killed in the process or who would irrationally choose to partake of the processes...those who, though they go through the motions of 'volunteering,' are casualties of strain, pain, or narcotics to such an extent that they really know not what they do...
>
> "I submit too, that the possible radiation from the proposed legislation, e.g., involuntary euthanasia of idiots and imbeciles (the typical 'mercy-killing' reported by the press) and the emergence of the legal precedent that there are lives not 'worth living,' gives additional cause to pause."
>
> Kamisar's voice helped raise a revival among Christian-taught orthodoxies, which broke out with strong sentiments against legalized murder. So much for quelling the tide in the 1950s and 1960s. That generation was faithful to promote life, but the worm was still in the apple.

Karen Ann Quinlan

By 1976, a landmark law case issued by the New Jersey Supreme Court declared that the overdosed Karen Ann Quinlan, unconscious and on life-support machinery, had a "constitutional right to die." The ruling gained added force when the U.S. Supreme Court declined to review their decision, thus agreeing with it.

A question remained, however. The father wanted the right to remove life-support equipment on behalf of his daughter. The patient herself could not consent to her own death, but could the parent as surrogate? They questioned whose rights were being protected.

The Quinlans (a Catholic family opposed to euthanasia) petitioned to have the respirator removed as "extraordinary care" but refused to discontinue fluids and tube-fed nutrition. "Clearly," opines Darrel Amundsen, "[the parents] perceived a distinction between extraordinary treatment that postponed death and ordinary care necessary to sustain life, a distinction that made a profound difference in this case when Quinlan confounded the medical experts by living on for nine years in a coma without a respirator."

The salient point that the Quinlan case brought into law is that it does not matter who the designated agent is in such a situation, but that *others* have an extraordinary extralegal power to bring death.

"At the beginning of the twentieth century, most people in the United States died at home without receiving medical treatment, and only a tiny percentage died in a hospital. Today, over 85 percent of all Americans die in a hospital, and in many of these cases somebody must make a decision to stop further medical treatment." —James R. Freis

---

There is no doubt that the increased medical technology of this century has prolonged life (by 50 percent from the last century) and presented novel opportunities to decide in areas where no decision had previously been imagined. Christian physician Rob Roy MacGregor, chief of the infectious disease section at the University of Pennsylvania School of Medicine, put it in historical perspective:

> "Until around 1900, there was very little a doctor could do to affect the course of any disease. The physician in that day was primarily a counselor and the interpreter of disease, conducting the patient through the course of the illness. Today he is a soldier—an aggressor against disease...a dehumanizing spiral [is set up] in which each organ failure is met by still another life-support procedure which they find difficult to understand or control."

As the right-to-die war raged, the 1990s saw the right-to-kill emerge. Americans and others began claiming a right to refuse extraordinary treatment, thus allowing the natural processes of death to occur without medical intervention. There were two reasons given for this:

(1) health care providers wanted to provide as little treatment as possible and to curtail end-of-life procedures

(2) the right-to-die could contain the exploding health care costs (the money, again) that threatened to engulf the Medicare/ Medicaid programs when the baby boomers grayed.

Patents on Humans

Along different lines, we have to look to where the moral dilemma originates. Should it be legal to apply for patents on human biological materials? Should patents be allowed solely for important medical research—or for any reason? This is possible now, and they are called "biopatents," issued by the U.S. Patent and Trademark Office (PTO).

Now we are faced with social-justice issues in allowing a governmental body to issue patents on living tissues belonging to the person from whom they have been confiscated, dissected, harvested, vacuumed, scraped from a petri dish, or excised.

Can we patent life and thus cavalierly change body-part ownership? Who actually owns *your* life? Are your body parts no longer yours after or during death? Can the wishes of your last will and testament be circumvented? Can one person's property (body) be sold or acquired by another so that it becomes the other's exclusive property—to experiment on, sell, torture, or even destroy at their will, even though it still contains living cells? This whole process flies in the face of God's sanctity of the human body.

Do you not know that your body is a temple of the Holy Spirit, who is in you, whom you have received from God? You are not your own; you were bought at a price. Therefore honor God with your body. (1 Corinthians 6:19)

The Council for Responsible Genetics has an interesting perspective in its opposition to biopatents. Look carefully at their reasoning and objections. What is behind their thinking? Is it economics, perhaps? A level playing ground for scientific research? Exploitation of the poor? Do they factor in spiritual consequences?

Patents make important products more expensive and less accessible.

Patents enable biotechnology and pharmaceutical companies to create monopolies in their products and lead to artificially high prices.

Patents in science promote secrecy and hinder the exchange of information.

The secrecy during the period of time between the filing date of a patent and the date the patent is granted tends to hinder the free flow of ideas. The fact that the PTO is significantly behind in processing patents extends this period of nondisclosure.

Patents exploit taxpayer-funded research.

Because most basic research begins in taxpayer-funded university laboratories, taxpayers are effectively charged twice for pharmaceuticals and other products—once when they pay their taxes and once when they purchase the final product.

First World patenting of Third World genetic resources represents theft of community resources.

Corporations in the industrialized Northern Hemisphere are raiding the genetic resources of the underdeveloped and poorer Southern Hemisphere, patenting those resources, and manufacturing products that are then sold back to the south at significant profit. Some have argued recently that this practice is a form of "biopiracy."

Patents on living organisms are morally objectionable to many.

Not only some religious groups but also many others find biopatents and the selling of living organisms problematic.

* * * * *

Let's consider our historic and traditional objection to legalizing the selling of human flesh and blood. The law of our land—specifically, the Thirteenth Amendment to the U.S. Constitution, states: "Neither slavery nor involuntary servitude, except as a punishment for crime whereof the party shall have been duly convicted, shall exist within the United States, or any place subject to their jurisdiction. "

Right now, according to the PTO, the whole human being may not be owned (by others) because of the Thirteenth Amendment. But this has not stopped them from allowing human genotypes (genetic structures) to be, legally speaking, patentable. Manipulating living organisms and calling it "creating (inventing) a living organism" is laughable in the least and certainly grossly offensive to the Creator who made all life.

When did *they* invent life? Or did they merely take a living thing, alter or manipulate its internal dynamics, and call it "an invention" so it could be patented and marketable? That which is invented grants the inventor the right to exclude others from the production, use, or sale of their new product.

You can imagine, though, the enormous power this can create when it is taken to its extreme.

The twisting of the Thirteenth Amendment, which has always excluded ownership of all that is human, circumvented the intention of the Constitution with the issuing of U.S. government-approved patents on human tissues. This opened the door to humans (via sale or donation of their tissues) becoming economic units of value by denying the value of life and property delineated by God. Thus, we have the subversion of the Bill of Rights, and a gray area is now black and white.

Brain Death and Euthanasia

The next section gives practical advice from Dr. Paul Byrne, physician, neonatologist, and expert on brain death and euthanasia. He outlines ways to not sign away your life:

Do not sign any advance directive that would deny you treatment on the basis of such vague and life-endangering language as the following artificial means benefit

- care appropriate to my condition
- incurable condition, irreversible coma

- inevitable and imminent death
- natural death, prolonging dying

Do not sign any advance directive that would deny you:

- life-sustaining or life-prolonging procedures
- heroic measures
- futile treatment

> *Note: All the terms above—artificial, incurable, imminent, futile, and the like—are simply too vague to interpret properly. So write your own statement, indicating that you want all possible care and treatment—period!*

This puts you back in charge of your life. Our recommendation is to not sign a living will or any of its variants, such as the Christian Affirmation of Life, and that if you have signed one, to rescind it in writing immediately and be sure to destroy every copy. Inform your family and friends.

Durable Powers of Attorney for Health Care (DPAs) became popular in the 1980s among the wealthy and allowed people to designate in advance who could make treatment decisions for them, taking the whim of medical and hospital staff out of the decision. "Thus," pro-life attorney James Bopp warned at the time, "(a) durable power of attorney is very dangerous, since there is no real limitation on the right of the third party to withdraw treatment or care when the patient is incapacitated."

Fortunately, living wills and DPAs never lived up to proponents' expectations, as Dr. Edward Larson tells us:

> "Studies indicated that although most Americans supported the concept of advance treatment directives, only 15 to 25 percent of adults completed them. Figures were much lower among minority groups and the poor. Hoping to raise these figures, Congress in 1990 passed a law requiring every hospital and nursing home in America to inform all incoming patients and residents about their rights to execute advance directives. Nothing worked.
>
> "'Even when patients have executed a written directive, they do not discuss that directive with families, the named proxy, or health care providers,' another research team found. 'Even the most detailed written directive is likely to be of limited value if there has been no communication among patient, provider team, and proxy decision maker...'
>
> "To clarify who possesses the right to refuse life-sustaining treatment for incompetent patients without advance treatment directives,

> several states have enacted statutes automatically giving this authority to the next of kin...Significantly, those instructions include the options of either receiving or rejecting life-sustaining treatment and offer a separate choice regarding artificial nutrition and hydration."

* * * * *

As I've written before and harped about on many radio programs, we Christians are not called to meet the world's expectations, fly to the moon without a rocket, or eliminate poverty. It can't be done, and we have higher orders, anyway.

So why do we buy into what the world legislates as solutions to their problems? The world might not want to care for the comatose child, the bed-ridden grandparent, the retarded teen who needs an expensive life-saving operation with limited projected success, the baby born without gray matter. That doesn't mean, however, that God will let us off these particular hooks.

What can we do? Can we love our neighbors as ourselves? We can do that, one person at a time. We can give them the gospel and tell them why we want to share spiritual food along with the casserole. Our lives have purpose and a positive direction that will not imitate nor embrace worldly wisdom.

We believers know that we are to hold our positions and not allow ourselves to be burdened by the slavish yoke of the world (and the devil). We are on active duty to bring the kingdom of Christ to the hope seekers.

CHAPTER 6

Ethics Revisited

Where do we Christians draw the line with genetic research and manipulation? With regard to abortion, some people draw the line at conception (no abortion for any reason) while others allow for the killing of the infant in cases of rape, incest, genetic maladies, and the health of the mother.

These last reasons account for about 7 percent of all pregnancies. Yet wholesale abortion is legally allowed up to and including seconds before natural birth in 93 percent of perfectly healthy babies and mothers. In these instances, no lines are drawn.

Technology is not the culprit. Many of us are alive and well today because of medical research breakthroughs. We must not confuse innovations like insulin, vaccinations, or penicillin with the destruction of human life at all cellular levels as a quest to improve medical science "for the good of all." When that happens, a very heavy line has been crossed.

Potential misuses of technology must be identified and averted from a moral posture, but who is able to contain biogenetic abuse? How will we know when it occurs if the people draw no lines?

Jesus regularly played the role of physician and healed many with genetic abnormalities. They were not hopeless to Him but valuable humans whose suffering He relieved and whose souls He died for.

Experimentation will continue to the absurd if no criminal restraints are put into place. For example, euthanasia is homicide and considered a crime. You go to jail for killing, no matter what the reason, as one male nurse found after the so-called mercy-killing of eight of his patients in a nursing home.

For waging war you need guidance, and for victory many advisers. (Proverbs 24:6)

It is to the benefit of the whole human community and especially for Christian doctors and biogenetic researchers to wrestle with the issue of genetics. To do this, you have to become familiar with what is happening in this rapidly expanding field, comparing what you see and hear with the study of the character and nature of God.

Would God tarnish the integrity of His Word, in which He established the gift of life as holy? Would He reverse His revealed will to save and preserve life, by granting the science gurus the right to willingly, ignorantly, and promiscuously devalue it?

Non-Treated to Death

On the Internet, Paul deParrie posts the back issues of a now-defunct magazine called *Life Advocate.* The magazine provides information about abortion and other bioethics issues. One article in particular served as an exposé of the kind of medical treatment offered in hospitals where you can be "non-treated to death." Here, he shares some of his thoughts on the peculiar way the medical community regards the whole issue of ethics.

> "If you are a Christian, your ideas are radical. The same is true of the unbeliever. We all live according to radical ideas. 'Radical' means from the center or from the heart and is the essence of all core beliefs. Ideas have consequences. Whatever you truly believe, you will act upon. I believe that God foresaw modern medicine's predicaments and supplied us with all we need to make rational, moral decisions.
>
> "And our moral decisions—Christian morality—are ultimately rational. As much as the unbelievers would like to convince you that only their core ideas are scientific and reasonable, this is not the case.
>
> "[The medical profession gives] the impression that medical ethics are somehow different from other ethics. The use of the word 'ethics' also implies that there was a

> moral decision-making process and that the conclusions are sound.
>
> "This impression is not true. Originally, medical ethics was simply how [Judeo-] Christian morality, or ethics, was applied to the singular practices and issues faced in medicine. But, because of the purported complexity of modern medicine, it is proposed that medical ethics can be different from the ethics we non-medical people are expected to live by. It is small wonder that some physicians develop god complexes. They think they are above ordinary rules (mores) governing mankind."

God has never been in the dark about how future medicine and technology would develop, and He has provided us with an absolute ethic in the Bible that can be applied to all areas of life. To think that the world has "new information" because they are looking at it "scientifically and reasonably" is absurd. What is right has always been right, and putting more stones in the pot will not improve the soup.

Christian ethics compete with secular ethics and always have—with some variations by both groups, depending on how close to the center each side slides. God's side doesn't move; the Bible doesn't change. It is the center of all, and by being on God's side, we are automatically at the opposite extreme of the secular worldview.

DeParrie gives some examples of competing core beliefs between Christians and the world. I've also added a few.

Christian Core Beliefs	**Pagan Core Beliefs**
God is sovereign	Man or nature is sovereign
"You shall not shed innocent blood"	Man, innocent or not, is expendable
All people are created equal	Some are more valuable than others
Care for orphans/sick/ elderly/needy	Survival of the fittest
God's right and wrong; absolutes	Situation ethics; there are no absolutes
God's Word is the whole truth	All beliefs are equal
Obey God above all Love one another	Do your own thing The betterment of society
Jesus died for sinful humankind	Man is basically good
Once to die, then judgment	Annihilation/higher planes/ reincarnation

---

"The custom of human sacrifice admits that the life of one is taken to save the lives of many, or that of an inferior individual is put to death for the purpose of preventing the death of somebody who has a higher right to live."— Nigel Davies, "Human Sacrifice" in *History and Today*

Living Wills

On the heels of this, what are the unbelievers (and undecided or uninformed Christians) doing to pull the plug on life? Why is there a plethora of living wills and no "living won'ts?"

Why do medical personnel and cash-hungry facilities insist on death alternatives instead of allowing people to die of natural causes? The pride of the world is such that it arrogantly feels competent and obligated to decide between life and death in certain "irreversible" or otherwise "hopeless" situations.

But how do *they* decide?

After years of getting the notion across that people will die painfully (and expensively—remember the money), hooked up to impersonal machinery, most states have been convinced to pass "living will laws."

Now we have the law to back up frightened, indecisive, emotionally drained family members and to convince future patients to sign away any hope of medical intervention on their behalf as they lay dying.

California became the first state to pass living-will legislation in 1976. Over the next fifteen years, vaguely written laws, varying from state to state, were rushed on the public, furnishing medical personnel with full liberties to interpret patients' wishes according to their principles. The American Association of Retired Persons—with its twenty-six million members—endorsed the trend, as did many mainline Protestant denominations. The Christian Church, outside of Catholicism, had entered the twilight zone of the slippery slope.

The Twilight Zone

OK. It's *your* last scene.

At 33 years old, you are lying in an immaculate hospital room. Your body does not have a square inch free from mechanical surveillance. Everything is measured, monitored, updated, calibrated, and flowing. Your brain waves suddenly go flat while your heart continues to beat strongly.

What do they do? "They," meaning the doctors and hospital executives, because your family doesn't know your wishes well enough to take you home to die naturally, or they don't care what happens either way.

People walk the halls. Should they operate again? Unplug and let you go? Starve and dehydrate you to death to free up a bed? Your blood work labels you a diabetic. Perhaps Dr. Jones will withhold insulin or withdraw hydration and nutrition for a few days. That certainly will make for a very painful death, although you appear quite tranquil due to the narcotics. The family thinks you look well considering the circumstances.

Again, after reading your living will (found neatly folded in your wallet by your unsaved cousin Geoffrey), your new doctor, whom you never met because you arrived unconscious, has decided to shorten your life.

One factor that nudged him in that direction was that the night nurse noticed the red organ-donor sticker on your driver's license inside your wallet.

Well, well, well.

After this point, there will be no alternatives

considered to save your life. That's all right with you. You had written that down during a college biology class when the professor had some handy little forms. You, and about twenty with you, signed over your last wishes. Now it was up to all these impersonal strangers to decide, remember?

But that was before you found Jesus Christ and really started living. That was so long ago that you forgot those items were still in your wallet, and now you believe in being healed by faith. How many times have you prayed for others?

Will they wait for your pastor to come pray for you? (You forgot to put that part in your wallet.) Ah, that depends. How fast do they want the bed?

Within two hours, a blue suit steps into your private room to gauge the length of time the hospital bed will be needed to keep you going. He thinks about releasing it for a more able-to-pay patient. After all, the monetary value between hanging on to you and, say, a possible complicated cardiac surgery is grossly different for hospital revenues.

You already picked what you wanted when you signed your living will! Besides, just think of all the *good* your organs will do for someone else.

The hospital ought to come out very well on this one, too. Before he turns to go, the blue suit calls the hospital's special "grief counselor" to work over your family…to prepare them. That's just to be nice, because they already have your organ-donor permission in their hands.

You faintly hear a voice to your left.

"Better start the fluids to preserve him long enough for organ harvesting."

As the room swims and dims, you wonder if they will do something to *save* your life.

* * * * *

Living wills in this sense are traps of Satan. They are instruments with vast latitude that allow others to make decisions for you when you can't.

Some doctors will interpret your living will to save your life. Others will interpret it to take your life. In either case, a living will does not recognize God as the One to make that decision.

And when the courts get involved because of a conflict between the hospital's wishes and the prolonging of the patient's life, anything can happen—and does.

Even when there are no living wills, the court might interpret that the patient wanted to have one and so sign the death warrant. This, again, is a clash between secular ideology and Christian core beliefs.

Check that ethics chart again to see how many collisions you come up with in deciding for your natural demise.

Chapter 7

Genetic Engineering Is Here

The connection of science with medicine has always been open to perversion, experimentation, and ungodly wealth gained from the sufferings of humankind. Robert Jay Lifton, M.D., author of *The Nazi Doctors: Medical Killing and the Psychology of Genocide*, put some of the pieces of the death-dealing philosophy together when he connected the art of medicine with the science of poisoning. From ancient times, some doctors have practiced in this way.

What is horrifying is that the "death-wish people" can be so organized, bureaucratic, systematic, cold-blooded, fraudulent, and deceptive in achieving their ends.

Here is a small portion of what Dr. Lifton discovered:

> "...the Nazis were not the only ones to involve doctors in evil. One only need look at the role of Soviet psychiatrists in diagnosing dissenters as mentally ill and incarcerating them in mental hospitals; of doctors in Chile serving as torturers; of Japanese doctors performing medical experiments and vivisection on prisoners during the Second World War...
>
> "...of South African doctors falsifying medical reports of blacks tortured or killed in prison; of American physicians and psychologists employed by the Central Intelligence Agency in the recent past for unethical medical and psychological experiments involving drugs and mind manipulation; and of the "idealistic" young physician-member of the People's Temple cult in Guyana preparing the poison (a mixture of cyanide and Kool-Aid) for the combined murder-suicides of almost a thousand people."

Medicine can be a religion, too. It has its own symbols (white lab coats, stethoscope at the neck, the snake-on-the-rod icon), while doctors serve as "medical priests" in patients' eyes.

In this technological age, these are powerful symbols we have come to regard as health-producing and lifesaving. The power of the "white coats" was not lost to the Nazi medical practitioners who left meticulous medical records that served so well later in their trials.

This is exactly what abortionists of today *do not* do: produce accurate, detailed, true medical records on patients. They do their dirty deeds and hide their tracks.

Here's an eyewitness account from Nazi Germany:

> "SS personnel manned the buses, frequently wearing white uniforms or white coats in order to appear to be doctors, nurses, or medical attendants. There were reports of 'men with white coats and SS boots,' the combination that epitomized much of the euthanasia project in general."

Looking to any powerful body—be it legislative, executive, judicial, medical, religious, or international—as the savior of humankind, is naive and dangerous.

Those of us who believe in one God, Yahweh Almighty, know better than to look elsewhere, because the search will inevitably lead to death for someone who does not fit into preconceived notions of perfection.

Playing God has immediate and long-term consequences, and it's better left to Him.

Testing and Abortion

Suppose you are a young couple in your late thirties expecting a second child. The doctor says you, the wife, are a little old for child-bearing and recommends prenatal testing, especially since your husband is known to be at "special risk" for carrying a specific disease gene found in his ethnic group.

Or perhaps you have a previous child or a relative with genetic abnormalities, or you have had multiple previous miscarriages.

"OK," you say. "Go ahead."

At first the prenatal testing methods are relatively noninvasive, such as ultrasound and blood sampling, but then it progresses to involve the use of much more invasive testing, like amniocentesis or taking samples of the fetus' tissues by invading the womb. Such tests carry risks for the termination of pregnancy of between 0.3 and 4.5 percent.

A small risk, you say? But this risk alone should alarm the expectant parents to decline further testing. It is possible *your* baby might be one of the 4.5 percent to die, all because of your curiosity. Fetal testing is done with the intention that if all is not well, abortion is the logical solution.

If you as conscientious parents have chosen to have your baby as the one God has given you, you do not need to submit to fetal testing. You will gladly take what God gives you.

Dr. Brock L. Eide relates that ultrasound may be used simply to help prepare parents for giving birth to a child with special needs or to allow for special precautions at birth where normal delivery would physically traumatize the baby. Scheduling a cesarean section would be wiser in some cases.

Let's briefly go back to the Human Genome Project at the Lawrence Berkeley National Laboratory. Project director Charles Cantor argued in a lecture that "the project would more than pay for itself by preventing the occurrence of just this one disease [preventing the birth of schizophrenics]."

We see right away what motivations he has—that of conserving funds and probably other hidden ones. A variety of other justifications have been offered for the practice of genetic abortion, but they come under three general suppositions: fetal benefit, societal benefit, and familial benefit.

It is up to each of us to decide if there are actual "benefits" to any of these groups that can conform to the sanctity of life position.

Under *fetal benefit*, the thinking is that the kindest thing one could do is to not allow a deformed baby to be born at all. Thus, the parents, armed with medical (and sometimes religious) advice, become the judge, jury, and executioners of their own baby, with the prestigious medical and legal communities in tow.

While many diagnoses have proven correct as to the condition of fetuses, some have certainly been unfounded and way off the mark.

Once the decision to kill is made, death is final and does not provide leeway for the Lord to intervene to heal the baby or bless the family with invaluable lessons learned in caring for a special-needs child. Playing God means that everyone except the baby decides what "quality of life" is and categorically rejects all options out of the ordinary.

The extreme to this position is that society deems it to be morally permissible (abortion is legal), morally commendable (it will help the fetus), and morally obligatory to go ahead and abort, since knowingly giving birth to a seriously impaired child could make the parents guilty of negligent child abuse.

You can readily see that submitting to fetal testing draws many more into the decision process than the parents, even to the possible justification (by the testing doctor) of interjecting a court system to intervene and possibly conclude that an (unwanted) abortion is needed.

After that, the next step would be to legislate to euthanize mentally or physically impaired infants, children, youth, and adults, because an assessment determined their quality of life fell below standards.

I wonder if former U.S. President Ronald Reagan would have been allowed the chance to have been born had a scientist detected his genetic predisposition to Alzheimer's disease. Who is to say that an impaired family member has no intrinsic value?

For we are God's workmanship, created in Christ Jesus to do good works, which God prepared in advance for us to do. (Ephesians 2:10)

With regard to *societal benefit*, you can imagine how the rest of the world feels about a "substandard" baby who would grow into a consumer of "limited" financial resources that the community has at its disposal.

The claim that such children would deprive others of scarce and costly medical resources is based on the idea that those resources demand a fixed, final amount—when in fact any amount of money can be raised for the disabled within the community as the issue is given attention and priority.

An interesting analogy of this possibility is made by Leon Kass:

> "Many questions can be raised about [such an] approach. First, how accurate are the calculations? Not all the costs have been reckoned. The aborted 'defective' child will in most cases be 'replaced' by a 'normal' child.
>
> "In keeping the ledger, the costs to society of his care and maintenance cannot be ignored—costs of educating him, or removing his wastes and pollution, not to mention the costs in natural resources that he consumes.
>
> "Who is a greater drain on society's precious resources—the average inmate of a home for the retarded or the average graduate of Berkeley? I doubt that we know or can even find out."

In the last justification for genetic abortion, it is argued in *familial benefit* that such a child would reduce the benefits of other family members by placing such a high demand on the family's time and money.

The thinking here is that a child has no value until it matures and is on its own, draining the family resources until that event. Then they ask, "How much worse would a disabled or retarded child be?" It is, again, the battle of secular thinking versus the sanctity of life.

The birth of a physically or mentally needy child into most affluent families today would bring depth and value to all the family members as they took their roles seriously and lovingly. Perhaps it is this lack of experience with suffering and serious illnesses that produces a society of self-centered people with an inability to respond patiently and steadily to the problems they encounter in life.

We must not forget that all humans are members of a great family, each made in the image of God (*Imago Dei*); that alone commands respect for all stages of our development, from inception of the first two cells all the way to natural death.

Artificial Reproduction

Radio host and author Kerby Anderson has done many shows on bioethics and biomedical issues. Below he has provided definitions for reproductive terms you're likely to encounter as you become more familiar with this issue:

> *Artificial insemination* is used as an alternative means of reproduction when male infertility is present. Today there are two types of artificial insemination: using the sperm of the husband (AIH: artificial insemination by husband) and using the

sperm of a donor (AID: artificial insemination by a donor; more popularly called DI, donor insemination). More recently, artificial insemination has also been used for female infertility. Women are impregnated with donor gametes (sperm and egg) so couples may adopt children born to these surrogate mothers.

In vitro fertilization (IVF) is used for female infertility. Conception takes place outside the womb, accounting for the popular term *test-tube babies.* The woman is treated with hormones to stimulate the maturation of her eggs. The eggs are removed and placed in a dish and fertilized with sperm. After a period of time, the developing embryos are surgically placed in the uterus.

Artificial sex selection, embryo transfer; and frozen embryos are other forms of artificial reproduction, including gamete intrafallopian transfer (GIFT), intrauterine insemination (IUI) in which thawed sperm is inserted by a catheter into the uterus; zygote intrafallopian transfer (ZIFT), a two-step procedure whereby eggs are fertilized in the lab and any resulting zygotes are transferred to a fallopian tube; and intracytoplasmic sperm injection (ICSI) in which the physician injects a single sperm into an egg, with the resulting zygote placed into the uterus.

Surrogate parenting is possible by using artificial insemination in which the husband's sperm is used to impregnate a donor mother.

Genetic engineering is possible through recombinant DNA (rDNA) technology. Scientists cut and paste pieces of DNA to completely redesign existing organisms. In the past, scientists were limited to breeding and cross-pollination. Now these powerful genetic tools allow them to change genetic structure at the microscopic level and bypass the normal processes of reproduction.

Cloning allows scientists to make multiple copies of any existing organism or of certain sections of its genetic structure. In the past, this genetic tool has been limited to simpler organisms, but the announcement of the cloning of a sheep suggests the possibility that cloning mammals (including humans) may be possible.

Genetic surgery and genetic therapy are developing techniques that will be used to treat and cure genetic diseases. Scientists can already identify genetic sequences that are defective and soon will be able to easily replace these defects with properly functioning genes.

The Food and Drug Administration has issued a "firm reminder" to doctors and researchers that they are required to inform federal health officials immediately of any deaths or serious side effects among gene therapy patients. The FDA responded just two days after the Washington Post *disclosed that scientists, drug companies and genetic research laboratories had purposely failed to notify the National Institutes of Health about six deaths that occurred as the result of their gene therapy experiments in the past 19 months. —From a news report*

---

* * * * *

Have you ever thought of the spiritual and moral implications of the above methods of artificial reproduction? Just the word "artificial" raises a red flag if we are trying to follow the character of God as revealed in Christ Jesus.

In the first case, *artificial insemination,* although adultery is not involved through sexually transmitted sperm, is it morally unacceptable when that sperm introduces a third party into the marital relationship? Artificially inseminating the wife with the husband's sperm is an unnatural method, but it is not sin in the biblical sense because the integrity of the marriage is upheld.

With AID/DI, a third party is introduced, so this method falls outside the sanctity and covenant of marriage. In using surrogate mothers—usually arranged through a business association—advertising is employed to solicit women who are then chosen by the couple because of physical and/or potential mental capacities.

The big problem with DI is that God's design is to beget children (through a married man and wife) who are genetically related to them, not to allow the husband's sperm to be united with an outsider's ovum. Couples attempting to produce a child with DI can never receive the fruit of their marital union.

Kerby Anderson asserts: "Adoption of a child already born and without a home is acceptable, while intentionally producing children who will require adoption by one or both spouses is quite questionable."

"I looked for a man among them who would build up the wall and stand before me in the gap on behalf of the land." (Ezekiel 22:30)

To Do or to Die

OK, You're desperate.

The Y sperm of your husband swims faster than his X sperm, and you always end up with a male child. That's fine, but you really want a girl after four tries. What should you do?

Some couples have used IVF to avoid genetic disease that might be sex linked, but the procedure is mostly used for sex selection. In China and India, money is not available for IVF, but the same rationale is seen.

First, the couple can decide to keep the "right sex" baby when it is large enough to identify its gender positively through ultrasound. Almost exclusively, the girl-child is aborted.

The next logical step in IVF after sex selection would be to screen for hair and eye color, skin tone, stature, and other physical characteristics. What do you do? You really want a daughter after four sons. Is IVF the way to go? And what if you find out it's a boy again after the testing is done?

The Bible announces that children are God's gifts (regardless of rape, "wrong race," incest, or gender). Parents who want to control "the gift of God" should consider their motives and the possible implications of such a decision to manipulate natural procreation.

In reality, artificial reproduction cuts across the sanctity of life in several ways.

First, there is the horrendous loss of fetal life—innocent human life. Some reproductive technologies are very inefficient and could result in loss of life.

Secondly, if the appearances of fertilized ova are "abnormal," the decision is often made to end those lives and try again.

Thirdly, in the practice of hyperfertilization, in which many ova are fertilized at the same time, only one is selected for implantation. The others are thrown away or frozen for "later use."

Remember that landmark fight by a divorcing couple in England over the ownership of their frozen fertilized ova a while back? One wanted them destroyed outright, and the other wanted total ownership. The courts had to step in. Imagine having any of *your* future children frozen for later use or simply thrown out.

God has the big picture in mind. He knows—and plans—the ratio of male to female across humanity, and He knows exactly what your family needs. Do we dare step into His shoes by selectively abandoning children?

Breeding for Beauty

This headline raises ethical issues for mainstream infertility groups, which expressed shock and horror at online auctions for a chance to breed for beauty.

One situation, as reported by the *New York Times* on October 23, 1999, involved a fashion photographer who began auctioning off the eggs of models. The transactions were done over the Internet, with prospective parents offering as much as $150,000 for the opportunity to have a physically beautiful child. The photographer used America's "celebrity culture" worship of beauty to justify his actions.

"If you could increase the chance of reproducing beautiful children, and thus giving them an advantage in society, would you?" he asks on his Web site. He sees the auction—with its "floating" prices based on perceived value—to be the natural outgrowth of the human desire to create a genetically superior people.

Infertility specialists around the country expressed outrage, calling the auction "unethical," "frightening," and "horrible." The photographer's actions, they said, were exactly the kind they were hoping the still-unregulated field of assisted reproduction would avoid.

"The worst part for me is to think there might be something worse still beyond our imagination," Shelley Smith, director of the Los Angeles-based Egg Donor Program, told the *Times*.

And the most frightening thing is, she's no doubt right.

Truth and Genetics

"When the moral boundaries are moved, tampered with, ignored, legalized, funded, and defended by liberal thugs, then any hope to protect the innocent is gone." —Drs. Bert P. Dorenbos

Theological and clinical perspectives must both be considered in the genetics area. William Cutrer, M.D., an ordained minister, has had to grapple with life and death issues from a Christian moral perspective. He suggests four foundational guidelines for dealing with these situations.

> *First,* erect the fence around the evil itself, not around the potential for evil. We should not necessarily oppose genetic engineering or genetic research. We should oppose that

which destroys life, and we should oppose the improper application of the knowledge gained.

Second, good applications, if they have come via information gained through unethical means, should give us pause. Having established the need to limit our own boundaries to those that we believe God Himself has given, we ask: "What are those limitations?"

Here are two:

• It is wrong to take a life.

• Life begins when the chromosomes align, creating a unique being—generally within the first six to twenty-four hours after the sperm penetrates the egg.

Third, life, even at the one-celled stage, has full personhood and the full rights of that personhood.

Fourth, we must leave room for the guidance of the Holy Spirit rather than specifically quantifying how much risk is acceptable in areas where there is Christian liberty. Life is messy. We seek to minimize the risk, yet we will never fully eliminate it, especially where medicine is concerned.

And completely outside of that, there is the area of personal conscience.

Chapter 8

To Clone or Not to Clone

The first crude attempt at cloning animals occurred in 1952 with researchers Robert Briggs and Thomas King, who started with the nuclei from the cells of frog embryos. They began with frogs because of their large eggs and ability to regenerate limbs. Their thinking was that perhaps this ability could be carried to regeneration of the entire frog.

Science advanced in other areas, and about twenty years later, cloning of pieces of DNA was begun at the molecular level of bacteria. In the mid-1970s when this was happening, a voluntary moratorium was imposed to sort out the ethics of cloning.

As this area became more exciting to researchers—and possibly lucrative to those who sponsor researchers—the self-imposed halt was lifted, and the universe of human cloning burst open once again.

But why clone anything, anyway? After experimentation with sheep proved successful in Scotland more than twenty years later, researchers developed an effective strategy to genetically engineer sheep for the production of pharmaceuticals, particularly a certain human protein or hormone in its milk. The human protein could then be harvested from the milk and sold on the market. But many, many complications had to be overcome to scale the hurdles.

Dr. Raymond Bohlin told me that it took 277 cell fusions to produce twenty-nine growing embryos; thirteen ewes were implanted, resulting in one pregnancy that produced one live birth. That is a miserable "success" rate of .36 percent!

That translates into nearly three hundred human embryos that would have to be sacrificed to possibly produce one "special" baby.

Genetically "Perfect"?

Other reasons to clone genetically perfected beings are related to the higher incidence of "bad genes." In ages gone by, people did not live long enough to develop and pass on genes that carried a weakness or possible disease. We are living longer, reproducing more, and passing down the hereditary "bads" with the "goods."

In the influenza epidemic of 1918-19, in which two of my father's siblings died, more lives were lost than in all of World War I. Infectious diseases like flu and typhoid are not genetically linked, but a higher toll is taken in people with genetic weaknesses who are sick, elderly, and very young.

Back to the bad genes. Suppose you were a person who inherited bad eyesight five hundred years ago. Nothing was wrong; you just couldn't see that well. One day during the hunt, a wild lion picked you off because you just didn't see it sneaking up on you. By the time you turned around, it pounced, and you were supper.

Later, eyeglasses and other remedies were invented to correct vision, and yet the inherited genetic eye weakness was still being passed on. Well, maybe pre-borns should be screened for sight weakness and eliminated outright. That would certainly help the gene pool in the long run!

Someday, when cystic fibrosis, cancer, Alzheimer's, and a host of other so-called incurable diseases have been worked on long enough, maybe we'll discover the key to turning them off—without eliminating little people.

Do we have the ethical fortitude to hold out for cures, or do we rush in headlong, tinkering with the genetic makeup, pronouncing certain weaklings beyond the pale of current science?

Is an Embryo a Human Life?

Dr. Raymond G. Bohlin has done extensive research into cloning. Here he attempts to separate fact from fiction and defines the difference between artificial twinning and cloning, which most people confuse.

"To clone a human involves the production of an exact copy of a previously existing individual...Identical twins are produced when a fertilized egg divides for the first time and, instead of remaining as one organism, actually splits into two independent cells.

"[Robert] Stillman and [Jerry] Hall were able to achieve this same effect by removing the protective layer around the developing embryo, splitting the cells apart, and replacing the outer with an artificial shell. Where there was once one embryo, there were now two identical one-celled embryos.

"To call this cloning, as the media has done, is a bit misleading. The more usual meaning of cloning an individual...would be to take a cell from an adult individual, remove the nucleus, and implant it in a fertilized egg that has had its nucleus removed. Strictly speaking, this was not possible with human beings at this time.

"Jerry Hall was asked if he feared that his work would create a public backlash toward this kind of research. He said: 'I respect people's concerns and feelings. But we have not created human life or destroyed human life in this experiment.' What this statement implies is that Hall and Stillman do not consider the embryos they were working with *as human life*.

"The embryos used in this research project were doomed from the start, because they

potentially "ill-defined crimes," is a formula for legal, and perhaps irreversible, nightmares and extreme consequences.

Addicts and Experiments

Pro-lifer and lawyer Elizabeth de Marees van Swinderen is an activist who is focusing her attention on the medical experiments performed on drug addicts. "This should be known by pro-life organizations and become a concern of theirs if we are to see progress in releasing the addicts from such a prison," she told me in 1999. Here is what she has to say about the situation in Switzerland:

> "The youth in Europe are very much endangered with the legalization of addictive drugs. Pro-life organizations [should] know that Switzerland has made plans for the prescription use of heroin for drug addicts who have applied for its use since 1993. This will gradually be followed with extensions.
>
> "The Netherlands is soon to follow. Preparations for experiments with prescription heroin have already taken the form in a basic document. The pope has said that we live in a culture of death, and these newest facts confirm this.
>
> "Twenty years ago it would have seemed impossible that such experiments would be widely and seriously discussed as an option.

> At that time, it would have been resisted as unethical experimentation on human beings. But there is no longer resistance from the Royal Dutch Medical Association, the largest medical professional organization in The Netherlands.
>
> "[This] experimentation endangers life, and it is the medical profession's responsibility to act as guard to the public and most certainly to the addicts themselves; such experimentation means killing on term."

The German Legacy

Law and politics are irrevocably connected. We have seen, through the German nation before, during and after World War II, what happens when God's force of righteousness—His church—does not stand together and does not stand for freedom.

In August of 1940, there were only eight hundred German pastors out of fourteen thousand who stood for freedom of religion, the others having signed Hitler's oath. These were the faithful. These are our legacy.

As Dr. Erwin Lutzer, the senior pastor of Moody Bible Church wrote: "The majority of Germans, including the professing Christians, no longer believed that Christianity was worth suffering for, much less dying for. They were willing to substitute *Mein Kampf* for the Bible in exchange for jobs and the greater glory of Germany. Yet those who saved their lives (souls) lost them, and those who lost their lives saved them."

The church is in these perilous times now with the threat of the formation of a worldwide government, the current persecution and deaths of Christians all over the world, and the holocaust against the pre-born and the elderly.

In early 1934 (the prosperous years), Christian activist pastor Martin Niemöller mounted his pulpit in a Berlin suburb and declared God's purpose in the trials that faced the German church:

> "We have all of us—the whole church and the whole community—been thrown into the tempter's sieve, and he is shaking and the wind is blowing, and it must now become manifest whether we are wheat or chaff! Verily, a time of sifting has come upon us, and even the most indolent and peaceful person among us must see that the calm of a meditative Christianity is at an end...
>
> "It is now springtime for the hopeful and expectant Christian church—it is testing time, and God is giving Satan a free hand, so he may shake us up and so that it may be seen what manner of men we are!
>
> "Satan swings his sieve, and Christianity is thrown hither and thither. He who is not ready to suffer, he who called himself a Christian only because he thereby hoped to gain something good for his race and his nation, is blown away like chaff by the wind of this time."
>
> —*Pastor Martin Niemöller (1944)*

I believe we are in the same times—and worse! For proof, Dr. Ingolf Schmid-Tannwald of Germany conducted a study on the current trends in politics, government approval, medicine and law, noting the parallels to the operations of the Third Reich in 1938.

Our apathy and approval of evil could lead us to even more horrendous consequences, since our capacity to destroy is impressively more powerful. Those with nuclear weapons, for instance, have manufactured enough to destroy the entire world seventeen times over, at last count—something even Adolph Hitler, Joseph Stalin, Mussolini, and Mao along with all their allies were incapable of doing.

But sanctify Christ as Lord in your hearts, always being ready to make a defense to every one who asks you to give an account for the hope that is in you, yet with gentleness and reverence." (1 Peter 3:15, NAS)

Dr. Schmid-Tannwald discovered fifteen criteria of comparisons for the Third Reich after 1939 and Today (1998). "In general, there was an identical correlation between what the Nazis commanded then and how we, today, measure up on life issues," he writes. "How does the culture of death affect us today? Just the same and probably worse."

Here is a chart based on his study:

The Third Reich and Today

	Third Reich-1939	Today-1998
Propaganda preparation	Yes	Yes
Approval scientific community	Yes	Yes
Selection process	Yes	Yes
Number of physicians	Approx. 42	thousands
Method of selection	Questionnaire	Prenatal diagnosis; on demand
Criteria	Not worth living /can't work	Unreasonable /unwanted
Person's consent to be killed	No	No
Informed consent of mother	No	Yes
Asst. physicians/nursing staff	Yes	Yes
Secrecy/misleading relatives	Yes	Yes & No
Legal basis	No	Yes
Approval by the public	No	Yes
Public funding	No	Yes
Killing in installations	only 10	Nationwide
Age of victims	Children/adults	Before birth
Collectively	Yes	No
Method of death	Death by gas	Surgical/medical
Killing becoming private	No	Yes/on demand
Killing of healthy humans	Racially Inferior	Unwanted
Adult euthanasia	Yes	Officially, no

This chart is chilling in its implications. We think history will not repeat itself and that all evil that has been done would be sufficient as a one-time event. However, it is even more awesome to think that we are living in more technologically advanced era when "to do evil" is so much easier.

"Rare and Safe"?

Mark Crutcher of Life Dynamics, an undercover investigative pro-life organization, has revealed many facts concerning the legal ramifications to abortion victims and the judicial environment in which the families of slain women have tried to pursue legal recourse.

Gaining legal victories is an uphill fight, and most legal battles fail in spite of massive malpractice evidence. Reportedly, "eight times as many women suffer an injury from medical negligence as there are malpractice claims."[15]

These types of cases are referred to as ABMAL—Abortion Malpractice suits. Let's look at a few case studies to get a flavor of the type of death and mayhem that is going on in the "rare and safe" abortion industry.

> **Case #189.** After her 1981 abortion, "Naomi" had to have portions of three fingers amputated because the drugs she was given were improperly administered.
>
> **Case #184.** "LaVerne," thirty-five and the mother of two, underwent an abortion at a Washington, D.C., area abortion clinic in November 1987. The nurse improperly placed a tube for anesthesia in her esophagus instead of her trachea. Before the mistake was discovered, the oxygen supply to her brain was cut off, leaving LaVerne in a permanent vegetative state.

Case #200. "Synthia" underwent an abortion and tubal ligation at an abortion clinic. According to a subsequent medical investigation, the abortionist "performed a surgical incision at a time when the operative field was not clear and the organs at the site of the incision were not clearly visible. He severed an artery; severed a vein; failed to locate the source of bleeding and hemorrhage; failed to stop the bleeding and hemorrhage; failed to summon help in a timely manner; refused to allow trained and skilled paramedics to attend to Synthia; he refused to allow paramedics to transport Synthia to a hospital in a timely manner; refused to follow medical advice from medical personnel at [a local emergency hospital] who requested immediate transfer of Synthia, and allowed Synthia to bleed to death."

There was also evidence that Synthia's medical records were altered, and based on additional evidence that these medical records were about to be destroyed, a court order was requested to preserve them. Synthia's autopsy revealed that she was *not* pregnant. She was twenty-four years old and the mother of two children.

Case #176: During her June 1979 abortion at an Atlanta abortion clinic, "Angela" stopped breathing. The clinic's nurse-anesthetist left another patient, "Delores," to attend to Angela. Unfortunately, she forgot to turn off Delores' anesthesia drip. Delores then went into cardiac arrest. Another staff member attempted to revive her with oxygen and intravenous fluids. However, she would not release her to an ambulance until the facility doctor arrived, resulting in a thirty-minute delay. Delores, who was fifteen years old at the time, went into a coma and was finally transported for emergency care. We were not able to find out if Delores recovered, but we were able to find out what happened to Angela. On June 11, 1979, at the age of nineteen, Angela died after spending a week in a coma (*Atlanta Constitution*).

"Teresa" underwent an abortion, during which she was told that her pregnancy was more advanced than the ten to twelve weeks previously estimated, [closer to] fourteen weeks. [The doctor] requested an additional $225, which Teresa did not have. He stopped the abortion and sent her home, still bleeding. Teresa was admitted to a hospital later that day, and labor was induced to expel a fetus missing a leg and its intestines."—Dayton (Ohio) *Daily News*

At a New York abortion facility, the abortionist had his license revoked because he "repeatedly perform[ed] 'abortions' that were not medically indicated, without ascertaining or attempting to ascertain whether patients were pregnant." The district attorney said 25 percent of the patients who underwent abortions in this clinic may not have been pregnant. *The New York Post*, which investigated these allegations, reported that this abortionist and his wife "tricked women who were not pregnant into having phony abortions."

These are just a few of hundreds of documented cases that are available across the courtrooms of America. Mark Crutcher, in his book *Lime 5*, addresses these issues and now investigates the sale of aborted babies' body parts to research laboratories. Of course it is "illegal" to sell human body parts, but the lines are blurring in the frenzy to fund "cutting-edge research" for other diseases.

Following is a portion of a radio interview I conducted with an unnamed pro-life activist.

> **Laurel**: Is it difficult for women who suffer physically from botched abortions to get legal redress?
>
> **Activist**: Yes, there are many barriers. The first one is the woman's attitude toward the abortion itself. It isn't unusual for them to insist that if they can't get help and keep it a secret from family and friends they depend on, then they will just have to "live with it." Additionally, if they were coerced into the abortion, they may find it even more difficult to disclose their injuries through a public lawsuit. One of the bitter ironies is that most of these girls live in a state where they can legally get an abortion without parental

knowledge, yet when they are mutilated during the abortion, they cannot get medical treatment or seek legal redress without the consent of their parents. Another big hindrance is their belief that "Maybe I just got what I deserved for killing my baby" or "God is punishing me for what I did."

Laurel: Are [they] aware of what an abortion entails and that it is a surgical procedure carrying great risks?

Activist: Ignorance and deception are the allies of the abortionists in these cases. Most ABMAL victims are from lower socio-economic backgrounds and don't even perceive that the judicial system is available to them [or] victims don't file suit because they've been convinced they can't. Abortion providers typically require their customers to sign a consent statement agreeing not to sue if something goes wrong during the procedure. From a legal standpoint, the document they sign is not worth the paper it is written on, and the abortionist knows it. But the girls don't.

Laurel: It seems that the victim is not protected by laws [that] punish the ones who deserve it most.

Activist: Besides that, the defense attorneys sometimes put the client on trial for her behavior. This is what they call "the Slut Defense" that has been so successful in rape cases. It is a cowardly way of disqualifying her as a person deserving compensation and tried in virtually every case. Defense attorneys will use every trick in the book to make her as unattractive as possible. Another defense tactic is the "Dead Baby Argument," by which he convinces the jury that "she got what she asked for—a dead baby—so why is she complaining?"

The client may be reluctant or unable to travel to the courthouse, or she is sometimes made to contribute financially to an attorney who calculates if the value of a settlement will match his efforts. An ABMAL case can easily cost between $25,000 to $50,000 before the first day of trial—not counting attorney fees. Only 29 percent of all medical malpractice cases that go to trial are concluded in favor of the plaintiff, and it may be extremely difficult to collect even if a judgment is brought against the abortionist.

Laurel: Do abortionists carry a lot of malpractice insurance, as regular medical doctors do?

Activist: A relatively high percentage of abortionists choose not to buy malpractice insurance at all. Then, if sued, they shield their personal income by declaring bankruptcy, hiding their assets in another country or putting them in a family member's name. At that point, the suit is worthless, regardless of how severely the woman is injured, because there is no money to collect even if she wins.

Another problem is that the abortionist will misdiagnose the state of the pregnancy and botches what is actually a second- or third-trimester abortion. Then the insurance company can legally refuse to pay the injured woman. This situation often arises when the doctor intentionally underinsures himself in order to lower policy costs and then intentionally underestimates fetal age in order not to lose a sale.

Laurel: Does [informed consent] help the victim or hinder her?

Activist: Informed consent has two parts. First, the patient must have enough information concerning the material risks, benefits and alternatives to the abortion so that she is able to decide whether or not to consent to the procedure. If the abortionist does not provide this information, he may be liable for inherent injuries. Then there is "material risk," which are risks that are "reasonable according to professional practice standards." In doctor-oriented states, if she gives her consent, it will not be with the knowledge that she might have her uterus perforated unless the abortionist believes that a perforated uterus is a "material risk."

Since few consent forms contain all the information the woman has a right to receive, it will be difficult to prove other than by her testimony that she was not actually given all the required information before signing the form. She will not know whether the abortionist has fully disclosed all the information on every material risk, since she is depending on him to know what those risks are. Yet, by simply introducing the form as evidence, the abortionist can show in court that she gave her "informed consent."

The defendant abortionist may argue that the injured woman was negligent in some way and contributed to her own injuries. For example, if the woman did not follow post-abortion procedures to the letter, the doctor may escape liability even if the injury was not related to a lack of follow-up care.

The devastating psychological consequences may never be compensated for.

* * * * *

Another issue of hot concern in the world today, much more pronounced outside of North America and most of Europe, is that of human rights. We will be looking at various conflicts between God's gift of freedom and man's abuse of humanity.

We should never underestimate the power of concentrated spiritual warfare prayer in these difficult places. When we can do nothing humanly possible against the greatest of obstacles, we always have a heavenly Father who sees and knows all. Liberty Savard teaches us to do this in her book *Shattering Your Strongholds:*

> "As I pray for others, I have a basic outline for binding and loosing prayers. To hold them steady, I bind (the positive, helpful side of binding) the individual (or nation) to the will of God, the truth, the blood of Jesus, the mind of Christ, and the work of the cross.
>
> The next step is to tear down the strongholds in the lives of the captives. This is vital to keep them from cooperating with the enemy's attempts to recapture them. You can pull them out of the fire, but you have to continue loosing their strongholds to keep them from voluntarily returning there. Continue loosing until the Holy Spirit reveals they have begun to take over the reins of their own deliverance.

We are in a spiritual battle, although we often see the physical faces of inequity, hatred, murder, and injustice.

Next, we will learn of practical ways of resisting tyranny while we witness the courage of those who face genuine hardship in obtaining basic human rights. One of our responsibilities is to intercede for those on the frontlines of the hottest battles.

Chapter 11

Human Rights and Active Faith

The Sale of Human Rights

The science and sale of life not only involves the buying and selling of living tissues extracted through scientific means. The sale of life is spoken of in Revelation as what the merchants of the earth deal in. What were they buying, trading and selling? After a long list, it ends with "bodies and souls of men."

These are human rights issues.

When we bring the kingdom of Jesus Christ near, there are many results. Releasing the captives, whether Christians or not, turns people to God and brings justice.

Taking the gospel to the nations is only the *outcome* of what must first be done to make the ground fertile to receive the gospel. Sometimes it means providing freshwater wells, food, and medical and dental relief. Some missionaries have put years into making friends, translating scripture texts, teaching literacy, delivering babies, and feeding prisoners.

"Nothing in the Bill of Rights promises that the freedoms there guaranteed can be enjoyed in comfort or a serene atmosphere...[D]iscomfort has always accompanied speaking on controversial matters. But if freedom is to amount to anything, one must be ready to pay the price." —Henry M. Wriston

---

There are as many ways to "prepare the way of the Lord" as there are situations of desperate need in places that do not know liberty or inherent human value.

I recently wrote a letter to Dr. Paul Marshall, who brings life and hope to the very real victims of human rights violations. He is the author of *Their Blood Cries Out,* which documents sufferings of many Christians in third World countries through the tragic violation of the God-given human rights; some even have lost their lives for the cause of Christ.

Taken from *The New Yorker* in 1993, the following article describes the army's reaction to a Christian girl from El Mozote, whose worth the Lord treasures.

> "There was one in particular the soldiers talked about that evening...a girl on La Cruz, whom they had raped many times during the course of the afternoon, and through it all...this girl had sung hymns, strange evangelical songs, and she had kept right on singing, too, even after they had done what had to be done, and shot her in the chest.
>
> "She had lain there on La Cruz with the blood flowing from her chest, and had kept on singing—a bit weaker than before, but still singing. And the soldiers, stupefied, had watched and pointed. Then they had grown tired of the game and shot her again, and she sang still, and their wonder began to turn to fear—until finally they had unsheathed their machetes and hacked through her neck, and at last the singing had stopped."

This is how Marshall begins his book on the human rights and religious violations of Christians worldwide. During our interview he said that he had taken up the subject of human rights after completing his doctorate some fifteen years earlier. He was philosophically interested but knew he needed to experience the actual practice of human rights in the world.

In the early 1990s, some Christians asked Paul to look at the persecution of Christians. He started with brief reports and small newsletters from organizations as Open Doors and Voice of the Martyrs. He correlated reports from others, Human Rights Watch and the Puebla Institute, traveled to many of the countries suffering and so began to write analyses and work with professional reporters for News Network International about events around the world that barely got a mention in other news media.

Why did so few know of these things?

In a powerful introduction to Marshall's book, Michael Horowitz exposes us to persecution by one who knows of it firsthand, having lived in a concentration camp. He begins his diary like this:

> "The mounting persecution of Christians eerily parallels the persecution of Jews, my people, during much of Europe's history. Today, minority Christian communities have become chosen scapegoats in radical Islamic and remnant Communist regimes, where they are demonized and caricatured through populist campaigns of hate and terror.
>
> "As ever, shrewd tyrants understand that their survival depends on extinguishing the freedoms of communities that live beyond the reach of the bribes and threats on which their power rests. Modern-day tyrants further understand that terrorizing the most vulnerable and innocent best helps them achieve power over all."

The ignorance and silence displayed by Western Christian communities toward the suffering of fellow believers completes the litany of parallels to earlier sordid chapters of world history. Despite all, there is a powerful reason why today's anti-Christian persecutions might continue to be denied, appeased, and silently endured by the world at large. Marshall writes:

> "The, 'Why, I never knew' excuses will be permitted to serve 'civilized' men and women well after the Sudanese holocaust has completed its course; well after Pakistani 'blasphemy' and 'apostasy' witch hunts have cut far-deeper swaths; well after the last Saudi Bible study group has been caught and tortured; well after the last Iranian evangelical bishop has been assassinated; well after tens or hundreds of thousands, perhaps even millions, of House Church worshipers in China have been beaten, jailed, and murdered."

The reason is *ignorance*, and it is fostered by preconceptions and conventional wisdom that lead many in the West to dismiss the fact of anti-Christian persecution as improbable, untrue, and impossible.

Here, as so often is the case, truth can become a victim of expectation and reality a casualty of prior beliefs. It is a lack of information that has for so long caused Western Christians to be so inactive regarding the suffering of their fellow believers.

Religious Persecution

When a poor but compassionate nation such as Ecuador takes in those forced out of rich America because they were refused asylum—namely, the Chinese emigrants of the *Golden Venture*—we must wonder where our priorities as a nation reside. And why, after years of accepting "the poor, the homeless, the tempest-tossed," can interests of a political party's unethically obtained campaign funds—from China—win out?

Human rights activists tell of a spiritual plague; massacre, rape, torture, slavery, beatings, mutilations and imprisonment. There are patterns of extortion, harassment, family division, and crippling favoritism in employment and education that affects more than 200 million people, with an additional 400 million suffering from legal impediments to justice.

Those who forsake the law praise the wicked, but those who keep the law resist them. (Proverbs 28:4)

World hatred and persecution is not about women, though most of those suffering are women. It is not about race, though the vast majority is black and brown and yellow. It is not about political activism, though many fight for freedom and human rights. It is not about war, though there are wars enough included.

It is not about terrorism, though terrorists wreak much of the damage. It is not about indigenous people, though it involves millions of them. Nor is it about famine and disease. These merely add to the suffering described here.

It is about persecution—*religious persecution of Christians*—and a story that is all but ignored and unknown in the world at large. Here is another true-to-life story one witness tells:

> "In Sudan on January 2, 1995, the village of Wud Arul, about two kilometers north of Sokobat, was attacked. Raiders came at dawn, storming through the whole area, looting and burning homes to ashes; kidnapping women, killing old men, women, children, and even babies.
>
> "About 150-200 men came, some on horseback, some on foot, and took away sixty-three women and children, as well as four hundred head of cattle. The women and children were taken via Um Ajac to either Meyram or Abu Jabra. Then they divided the captives up. Some were sent to the market; some were to be used for forced labor in agricultural work; young women were to become concubines; older women to become domestic slaves.
>
> "On arrival at Sokobat, we were greeted by the chief with a warm welcome. 'We are so glad to see you here. Often people come and say they will return, but never do. It is good for us to know that people do know about us,

that they care and that we are not suffering with no one knowing about our tragedy.'[12]

Comfort Zone of the West

Before leaving this area of concern, we should address the "consumer Christian mentality" in primarily Western nations where personal well-being, a constant search for comfort zones, the aversion to controversial subjects, and the hope that Jesus died for our problems and not for our sins abounds.

Many Christians who do not strive for kingdom interests out of personal obedience spend their lives trying to attain personal success and high financial goals. They are likely to be enamored of biblical diets, social events, men's football nights, and "Christian entertainment" at their meetings.

There is also an indulgence in "Christian psychology" to answer soul concerns. These time-wasting activities leave lukewarm believers frivolous to societal issues, happily uninformed, and immersed in introspective pursuits.

"The church must not only teach righteousness, it must actively resist unrighteousness. Resistance *is* activism." —*Randall Terry*

Why hasn't this type of Christianity worked in other nations—for instance in Sudan, China, or Vietnam—like it works in the West? Why have the persecuted "failed" in comparison to wealthy Western Christians? The material wealth is not there, yet these believers continue to stick with God, as shown by their vibrant faith and underground meetings.

Indeed, the Apostle Paul wrote from prisons. Jesus was markedly unsuccessful in today's terms. He didn't own a home, a wardrobe, or mode of transportation, or come from a prominent family. Instead, for His good works He was betrayed, abandoned, and finally hanged naked on a cross to die painfully.

Where was His guarantee of "peace"?

CHAPTER 12

Medical Ethics

Of all those involved in sanctity of life issues, Christians in the medical profession face the greatest and most painful challenges, as they seek to practice their medical calling and earn a living for their families.

Why? Because the bottom line of life and death strikes where doctors must make final decisions in the health care of others. Medicine never used to be so nebulous or controversial. Doctors took the Hippocratic Oath and promised with all their skill, knowledge, will, and experience to save lives to the best of their educated abilities. Medical people are essentially lifegivers, lifesavers and life preservers who do not regard their patients' age, gender, race, financial ability, religion, or quality of life as a basis for treatment.

Nurses, too, face a new dilemma: They may be called on to perform procedures some doctors hesitate to do in case of legal repercussions. And now, in some countries, relatives have the power to "pull the plug" on an elderly or disabled family member when they want to—even when medical prudence would hesitate or advise differently.

We are going to read some of their stories, their anxieties and their experiences in clashing with popular culture. They are in the crunch with national politics, family wishes, and international agendas that can now reach into their nations, regions, hospitals, and patients' lives. It gets personal. And these are life and death determinations.

"Why should I have to become an executioner because the government now allows for abortion?" Dr. Albertus van Eeden from South Africa asks. "I cannot kill a baby no matter how legal it is and should not have to lose my profession over it."

Good reasoning.

The Dark Side of Medicine

Doctors have had to agonize over these issues, sometimes years before the rest of us even hear about things like physician-assisted suicide, euthanasia, partial-birth abortion, genetic engineering, medical experimentation, fetal tissue use, pre-implantation diagnoses of embryos, commercial organ harvesting and many more related procedures.

Medically speaking, abortion is a sleazy and offensive procedure. A doctor who does abortions—even if they are only a small part of his or her practice—is known as an abortionist. This label is supposed to be the kiss of death for any professional hopes they might have.

Even practicing abortionists admit to this reality. As

soon as abortion became legal in 1973 (in America), Bruce Stier came under attack, because it was known that he would be performing abortions. He recalls that as he was scrubbing up one day shortly after the *Roe v. Wade* decision, a colleague standing next to him asked, "So, Bruce, how many babies are you going to kill today?"

Abortionist Morris Wortman says, "Abortion has failed to escape its back-alley associations." In his mind it is still treated as the "dark side of medicine...Even when abortion became legal, it was still considered dirty."

Finally, a Florida newspaper quotes abortionist Robert Crist, who was lamenting that some physicians who don't do abortions treat him "like a second-class citizen." Some of the ones who do—especially the younger, inexperienced ones—have admitted to an increasing level of discomfort. Crist says he knows of others who have quit because "the stigma had become overwhelming."

Abortionists who haven't killed a patient, or turned someone into a vegetable, see themselves as the abortion industry's elite. And while they may be right, that seems like a pretty low standard to set for themselves and their profession.

In the next section, I've included some medical papers from doctors. With persistence, we will get into the deeper philosophies of the medical underpinnings for today's technological answers. Medical personnel must arrive at biblical decisions regarding career, morality, clear conscience, and obedience to the Lord Jesus at all costs. Sometimes, that is very costly.

Here is where pro-life lawyers and doctors make a wonderful team in changing law in the health care field to protect life.

"We should be characterized by giving, not withholding. Christ has called His own to give all, in order to win all."— Dietrich Bonhoeffer, in a comment critical of the Church when its only interest was self-preservation.

A "Technological Spirit"

A medical paper on "The Threat of Euthanasia" was handed to me at an international conference. It was written by a pro-life Dutch medical doctor and member of parliament, Dr. Egbert Schuurman, and it gives an excellent summary of the philosophy behind areas of unethical medical research.

> "Generally speaking, the most physically deformed fetuses will be selected for abortion. This tendency will be replaced in the near future by selection of the best embryos obtained via in vitro fertilization. The rest of the human embryos will be destroyed or used for scientific experiments.
>
> "This grotesque development is possible thanks to the latest results of the Human Genome Project in Holland, in combination with

information technology. All pro-lifers—all of us—need to give attention to this lawless development.

"The mainstream of our culture is, in my opinion, dominated by technocism, or better said, 'a technological spirit.' In this light, it seems clear that the ideal of scientific technological control stamps itself upon all in the culture.

"If the same humanistic bedrock is active in relation to prenatal diagnoses and pre-implantation diagnoses, then developments in medical practice cannot help but have a destructive influence.

"The main trend in our culture is marked by humanistic religiosity. Humankind, as master, seeks victory over the future. He wants to have everything his way and completely centered on his wants and needs. He desires to solve problems old and new and to guarantee as a probable consequence, material progress.

"Technocism always implies that there is an obstacle or enemy in its way. It may be God, or nature, another country or state, or competitors. In the case of abortion and euthanasia, human life itself is viewed as an enemy.

"Everything is reduced to a technical object, with technology in control. In such a man-centered universe, we are no longer left to love God and love our neighbors.

"Man without God means that other gods and lords that become 'masters' over God's creation must replace God. Man wants to create a worldly paradise, a paradise that can be manipulated technologically. In the meantime, the perspective of eternity is certainly lost. Heaven is closed and so is hell. Given the split between the divine world and earthly reality, man has set his heart on technology and its resulting benefits.

"This mindset is the religious driving force behind our present technological society and is enormously stimulated by welfare politics. If Christians are not aware of this religious background, they really lack the capacity to offer an adequate critique of our technological culture and to indicate the direction to go, which is God's way."

Dr. Schuurman now turns to a discussion of prenatal diagnosis:

"There are several methods of prenatal diagnosis. If in that process a disabled fetus is detected, for instance with Down syndrome, then abortion mostly follows. Nevertheless, a lot of disabled children have been born. How do we resolve that in our culture?

"From the standpoint of technocism, human procreation is very ineffective and inefficient.

When the Human Genome Project is finished, it will be possible to detect more than forty genetic failures that are said to cause genetic disease during the human lifetime.

"Hav[ing] babies that are physically or technically "nearly perfect" will be [accomplished] by selecting the "best embryo" to implant via in vitro fertilization. Then a baby with a technical qualification can be born.

"Some negative consequences of this development mean that a lot of human 'best embryos' will be destroyed or used for scientific experiments before their destruction. Human life will most certainly be devaluated to the level of technological standards of bad—good—best. Human beings will then be able to be born with a "technological guarantee."

"The idols of technology and economics are making a lot of victims for the future. The future seems not to end in a technological paradise, but in an enormous chaos of selective death.

"The struggle of the pro-life movement will be a heavy one, but at the same time, it will become clearer that the selection process for human embryos leads to the process of eugenics with an open end to unlimited destruction of life. Living in faith and hope and acting in love means that we are free from technocism and made responsible for healthy directions in health care."

"Our challenge is to live and speak the revolutionary truth that Christ died so that He could destroy death and overcome Satan, the actual destroyer of worlds, and rob the grave of its victory. Our culture dances with the 'prince of death,' because it does not know the Prince of Peace." —Craig and Janet Parshall, Tough Faith

---

"Active Help in Dying"

Here is a second opinion, from a German doctor this time—Anneliese Funnemann, the director of Right to Life Seminars. She describes a brush with Australian bio-ethicist and pro-death philosopher Peter Singer.

> "In post World War II Germany, the word 'euthanasia' until recently was taboo. It raised bad memories and emotions and perhaps also feelings of guilt about what had been done to mentally ill people during the Nazi regime. In the West, one risked severe criticism if they even used that word.
>
> "Although the word euthanasia was stained, it was possible to talk about using 'active help in dying,' but it all came down to exactly the same thing: schizophrenic murder! Currently there are two organizations that propagate active help in dying. One is the Humanistic Union and the other is The Society for Humane Dying. This last one began some years ago on the wrong foot,

as it had provided and sold cyanide tablets for profit making.

"In 1986, a draft of a law for help in dying, drafted by a workshop of doctors and jurists, was published. This draft has as its basis the following:

"The patient should be able to experience dying as part of his self-expression. For 'killing upon request,' the doctor should go unpunished. The unconditional protection of a person trying to commit suicide should no longer be a medical obligation."

"Hidden from the public but intensively discussed in medical circles and at conferences are the 'new ethics' of the Australian bio-ethicist Peter Singer. A medical conference in Bonn on the ethical and judicial consequences of terminating the treatment of patients in vegetative states was held in connection with Project Biomed, which I promoted through the European Union.

"In these patients, the function of the brain stem is still present. They breathe spontaneously and all reflexes are present, so the vegetative state functions as digestion. But they are not able to show any sign of self-recognition or recognize their surroundings.

"Several weeks ago, we were again confronted with Peter Singer's activities. The Institute of Heidelberg for Systematic Research had planned to have him speak. But due to a

> protest, the organizers of the congress were forced to refrain from allowing Singer to come to Heidelberg. However, he was connected by television.
>
> "Another time, his participation was prevented due to protest. Singer's thesis was summarized in the periodical for German doctors as follows:
>
> 1. The traditional ethics of the integrity of life had been broken. He said: 'The factor that pushes us strongest to a change is our increasing humane ability to keep persons alive.' He indicated that persons everywhere accept definitions of brain death as actual death.
>
> 2. There is a need for greater freedom for decisions concerning one's own life as demonstrated by the euthanasia rules in The Netherlands, which accordingly, were approved by 80 percent of the population.
>
> 3. The worth of human life is no longer valid under the criterion of sanctity but is now judged according to its "quality."

* * * * *

The giving up of traditional values in medicine is a dangerous development. On one hand, the physician becomes "the killing doctor" who helps to fulfill patients' wishes independently of his or her own conscience. On the other hand, doctors can declare living persons to be dead.

From Germany, we fly north to Lithuania and its brave citizens, who often fought alone for national sovereignty in the world wars. They are fighting in a new way now—still saving their citizens.

A Baltic Battlefield

The following was written by Alina Saulauskiene, M.D., president of a Lithuanian association of pro-life doctors. Dr. Saulauskiene writes:

> "The problems of the value of human life, inviolability, human dignity and human rights are very acute and hard to resolve in Lithuania. The harvest for life defenders is ample, but there are only a few workers. During over fifty years of Communist occupation, a mentality of materialism and Marxism was formed in the people's consciousness. The regard of man as of material origin without right to ownership, without conscience or rights of belief, has been binding our society.
>
> "Although we are a Catholic land and claim that 75 percent of us are Catholics, our lives are still impregnated with atheism.
>
> "The law on legal abortion at one's own will until the twelfth week of pregnancy is still valid (since 1955). Babies in eighty families have been fertilized in vitro during the last ten years as a result of the new Western medicine technology invasion.
>
> "The chemical contraceptives of the Western pharmacy firms have flooded our small country.

Their impertinent advertisements are encroaching on conferences, hospitals, and outpatient clinics through mass media propaganda.

"The International Planned Parenthood Federation (IPPF) organization in Lithuania, under the name Sexual Health and Family Planning Association, is carrying out all this dirty work.

"Our association unites 230 members, and 75 percent of them are doctors. In 1998, more than a thousand doctors and three hundred [medical school] graduates swore the original Oath of Hippocrates. We have arranged a series of conferences on medicine's morality and ethics in various towns.

"In Lithuania, the number of abortions performed annually almost equals that of births—about thirty-seven thousand. Recently, the number of both abortions and births was decreasing.

"Already for three years, the number of coffins has been exceeding that of cradles. Crosses and monuments for the unborn are built at the initiative of our association.

"We succeeded in stabilizing artificial surgical sterilization. The Ministry of Education and Science stopped the encroachment on schools by IPPF representatives. We affected a bill on in vitro fertilization and closely cooperate with the church on the solution of moral laws.

"The shortage of funds and specialists presents

the biggest problem. There are few enthusiasts—idealists who agree to work without wages. Lithuania is very short of money."

— *Alina Saulauskiene*

What About Prenatal Testing?

Prenatal testing is inevitably linked with both the larger issues of abortion and genetic testing in general. Whatever type of prenatal screening is utilized, the purpose for the screening must be examined.

Because prenatal genetic surgery is limited in its current applications, the usual option offered the prospective parents, when it is learned that the fetus is suffering from a genetic malady, is to abort. Thus, how one feels about prenatal screening and testing is inextricably bound up with how one feels about abortion.

To sharpen the dilemma, it is not unusual for physicians to exert pressure to abort by refusing to perform prenatal screening unless the couple agrees to the abortion if the genetic anomaly is severe. Insurance companies, hospitals, and HMOs can also exert pressure on the couple.

It is not uncommon for institutions to offer prospective at-risk parents the "choice" of either a paid abortion or the termination of their health-care benefits (forcing the parents to pay enormous costs of long-term care out of their own pockets).

When the choice is framed that way, it is really no choice at all.

"A host of tragic dilemmas arise because our ability to diagnose genetic disease has far outstripped our ability to treat."—Michael McKenzie, Genetics and Christianity

---

The next chapter goes into specific detail of those in the medical professions who are actively pursuing their calling and bringing ethical action to bear. We will get a look at the alternatives Christians (and others) have regarding death with dignity in God's timing. You will also meet other crusaders who will encourage you and offer examples of how you may participate in this quest for life.

Chapter 13

Medical Activism

In dealing with life issues for medical professionals, we must look into their world and see the options that have always been open to them, options that are being cut away legislatively and by world opinion, and options that are now making an impact on the way they live their lives.

A Study in Dignity: Dr. Francis Schaeffer

Francis Schaeffer's death offered an example of death with dignity, love, mercy, and peace. The decision came on Easter Sunday of 1984. Dr. Schaeffer, a world-famous champion of the Christian right-to-life movement, had been dying from cancer for several years. As his condition worsened, he had moved with his wife, Edith, from their long-time residence in

Switzerland to a new home near the Mayo Clinic in Minnesota. Extensive treatment allowed him to write and lecture to very near the end.

But when final treatment decisions had to be made, Schaeffer was no longer able to make them himself. A team of Mayo doctors called his wife aside, and the leading consultant asked her, "He is dying of the advancing cancer. Do you want him to be placed in intensive care on machines? Now is the time to make the choice."

Edith Schaeffer knew precisely what she and her husband wanted. "You men have already done great things during these last years and these last few weeks. You fought for life and gave Fran time to complete an amazing amount of work," she replied, reflecting on the distinction that her husband had drawn between preserving life at all costs and prolonging death. The time had come for her husband to go home, surrounded by the familiar things he loved.

Soon he was home, in a bedroom with a large window overlooking colorful flowers put there each day in pots, because it was still winter in Minnesota.

Treasured memorabilia from Switzerland filled the room, and his favorite music by the masters flooded their home. Ten days after leaving the hospital, amid the sounds of Handel's *Messiah,* Francis Schaeffer died without treatment that could have prolonged his life. His wife had made their home into a hospice.

The Hospice Movement

One of the greatest movements that came from England in answer to the right-to-die trend emerged in the person of Anglican physician Dr. Cicely Saunders, who studied under Oxford scholar C.S. Lewis before World War II.

While serving as a nurse during the war, she became particularly concerned about the terminally ill and what was happening to them. In 1967, she founded the first modern hospice, St. Christopher's, where she could develop a medical service (ministry) to the dying.

By the mid-1970s, the hospice movement came to America, and it provided access to pain relief without benefit of life-supporting assistance for only those with a determined, shortened period to live. It has since spread to many nations, with about one-third of all hospices sponsored by religious organizations that can provide the spiritual component.

Reducing the Pain

Dutch pediatrician G. van Bruggen offers this perspective on the care that can be given to children with Down syndrome:

> "A child with Down syndrome has two major problems. He or she is seriously handicapped and life expectancy is limited. These factors affect each other. Therapeutic interventions should be proportional; i.e., the burdens of care should not be heavier than the positive effects.
>
> "In the case of a dying child, many therapeutic interventions are disproportional. This means that all attention should be given

> to palliation and mitigation of suffering.
>
> "In this field, much is possible. If the child is hungry, feed him. When he vomits, do not force food. Why should he die with a filled stomach? Does he have convulsions?
>
> "There are numerous anti-epileptic medications to relieve this. In case of severe pain, choose from the many possibilities of controlling pain, such as the use of general medicine, local medication, or the blocking of nerves. Treatment is possible with morphine or methadone in line with the [accepted] guidelines. Also, an anaesthetic group or a neonatologist could be asked for expert advice.
>
> "If the child is dying during an adequate pain alleviation treatment, that would mean good terminal care is being given. It would be better not to prevent dying longer than would be necessary through extraordinary means, but rather to accept death as inevitable and natural.

A "Pool of Dreadfulness"?

Having a disabled child has been described as a double process: The (exact) child awaited did not come but what did come was a child with a lot of psycho-social consequences. There is often shock and shame, a disturbed bonding between parents and child, and the reaction of family members, grandparents, and friends.

The child lays a rightful emotional claim on the parents: "I belong to you!" A period of strong ambivalence in the relationship between parents and child follows. Many parents show feelings of rejection. Time and again doctors themselves show rejection behavior.

In The Netherlands in December of 1995, an important symposium, "On the Verge of Life and Death," attracted doctors, lawyers and ethicists. One speaker mentioned that it might be necessary to bring about the death of a child if its future meant being nursed in one of the severest departments of a well-known facility for the mentally handicapped.

He was asked if the patients already housed there should be killed. His answer was no, but he added that it would be preferable to end the lives of these newborns "because life will be worse than death." Why, then, withdraw such "charity" to someone who is already in that position? It makes no sense.

Moreover, disabilities are many times described by doctors as far more serious than that experienced by the patients themselves. A professional in pediatrics referred in court to children with Down syndrome as a "pool of dreadfulness," when in fact many of these children bring great joy to their families.

In the course of the day, it became more and more clear that some of those present wished that the disabled should die—not only the babies, but also older children. When speaking about a severely mentally handicapped three-year-old with pneumonia, one speaker said, "Let us be honest. We would very much prefer that the child dies as a result of this pneumonia." Others, however, would have tried to combat pain and relieve the tightness in the chest with normal treatment.

Pediatricians in The Netherlands agreed that treatment should only take place if and when it offers possibilities for a cure or care; otherwise, it becomes ill-treatment. However, they disagreed about whether the killing of physically or mentally disabled children is an option.

Besides this, an increasing number of pediatricians considered relieving pain not really meaningful. They preferred killing.

Pharmacists: Unlikely Crusaders

In 1996, the six-thousand-member California Pharmacists Association adopted a policy allowing pharmacists to refuse to fill prescriptions based on "ethical, moral or religious grounds." John Boling, a pharmacist at a California drug store, cited "moral objections and refused birth control pills for a woman wanting to practice a morning-after method to prevent pregnancy" [notice the newspaper's politically correct terminology, not to "self-abort" or "prevent implantation"].

A vice president for Planned Parenthood called the actions "horrifying" and said no third party has the right to intervene in a personal decision made between a woman and her doctor.

Time Magazine reported that "a recent survey of 625 pharmacists showed that 82 percent of them believe they have the right to refuse to fill a prescription for a drug such as RU-486 that would facilitate abortions. A new era of conscientious objection may be dawning."

Doctoring Death

Regarding the situation in France, Dr. Henri Lafont contacted me about a meeting held in Paris for medical and psychiatric professionals. Not missed on Lafont, an activist in an association of pro-life doctors in France, was the irony of the symposium's title: "Prenatal Euthanasia," or as Lafont called it, "a new word for an old technique."

He calls for a "very strong and definite language" when it comes to life issues.

"We should not talk of active or passive euthanasia; that puts us into confusion," he says. "We agree with the wish to die in the faith (euthanasia in an etymological connotation), but we should not kill anyone. Direct killing is outside of the elementary ethic of medicine.

"To die in comfortable conditions and with dignity is a normal wish for everyone. The aim of the medical practice is to assist the patient in this way. To care until the last moment must be the rule of every doctor; never put an end to the care that can be given."

* * * * *

There are quite a few nurses for life, too. They are often put in a position of obeying authority where the lines seem to get ever closer to—if not actually cross—the threshold of morality.

Imagine a pediatric or obstetric nurse watching or assisting in a partial-birth abortion. She or he observes the tiny body emerge as healthy, whole, pink and kicking, feet first.

Then, holding back the head from final delivery, the physician picks up a sharp instrument, locates the baby's spine, and cruelly jabs into it. The delicate, pulsating fluids erupt at the base of the skull, and the cord is irreparably severed.

The tiny body shudders. It is usually an almost full-term baby and not some "blob of tissue." This is all done without anesthesia to the child. The nurses watch the little arms flailing wildly, begging someone to rescue him as brain matter is vacuumed out.

A perfectly lovely baby that someone would want has become a lifeless body handed to the nurse for disposal. No name. No funeral. No shame or legal consequences. No compassion.

This is medicine?

Nurses and medical assistants are wonderful people. They are responsible to hold life and death in the area of their expertise and treatment. All their training is geared toward saving lives and caring for the sick. Infanticide flies in the face of all that.

In this last century, we have learned that doctors are not God: God is God, and there is a higher authority to answer to. Some nurses have formed pro-life unions finding strength in numbers and powerfully acting in hospitals, clinics, offices, medical emergency rooms, and all sorts of places to promote life, bring healing, and calm anxieties.

Here is a story by one such organization based in Malaysia:

"There is discrimination against women—especially regarding reproductive health—and the breakdown of family values. The human person is not being considered as central. There is an urgent need to strengthen the family to promote a culture of life, as well as to protest against all attempts to spread the culture of death.

"You may ask what you can do all alone, individually, at your own level of responsibility, in a world that fails to agree with your Christian vision of health. 'Who am I to speak up?' you may say, and 'No one is going to listen to me after all.'

"What you are unable to do by yourself becomes possible if you join forces with others to create a current of opinion, but each individual must decide to do something. This is our initiative. Together with other pro-life organizations, we can be in the forefront of facing these challenges.

"The message of the new millennium is clear. It is our vision of faith and the mission of love for human beings that will enable us to take bolder steps forward into the future. I wish all those participating in the pro-life cause on all levels, all across the world, to remain very courageous."

—Sir Richard Lai, Catholic Nurses & Medical Social Assistants

South Africa Speaks Out

In South Africa abortion on demand can be practiced until birth, although in theory, according to the new Termination of Pregnancy (TOP) Act, it is allowed on demand only up to twelve weeks gestation. Also, it is allowed from thirteen to twenty weeks if there is a serious risk to the mother; the fetus would suffer from severe physical or mental abnormality; the pregnancy resulted from rape or incest; or the mother's social or economical circumstances would be significantly affected. After the twentieth week of gestation, abortion is allowed for the first two reasons.

In the remainder of this section, Dr. Albertus van Eeden describes and comments on the state of abortion and euthanasia in South Africa.

> "Any citizen who deliberately takes the life of another is guaranteed a fair trial and a lawyer if he cannot afford one. He has the right to a balanced diet, the best medical care, exercise, a library, opportunity to study, and a counselor. He may even marry in prison and be given conjugal rights. He may protest or go on strike if he feels his rights are being violated. He has the right to protection from violence in prison and the right to a decent burial paid for by the state—and ultimately by the taxes of his victim's loved ones.
>
> "But an unborn child has no rights and is not protected by the state or our Constitution. The

rights of the child are passed on to the mother who can be as young as fourteen, with or without education, with or without a home background that at least provided some standards and values.

"That teenager is too young to vote, too young to sign a legal document, to open a bank account, get a driver's license, to apply for her own passport or to be served alcohol. She is barred from certain movies that show too much violence, rape scenes and/or explicit sex, yet she has the right to demand without the knowledge or consent of her parents that the life of her unborn child be terminated.

"Since the TOP Act was passed, more than forty-five thousand children have been aborted in South Africa alone. The National Alliance for Life has been formed as a loose umbrella where pro-lifers plan activities together on a national level. We look upon the general population as our main target.

"We have found that it is a more healthy way to work from the bottom up than from the top down. Because of that, we put a lot of emphasis on educating and influencing the public by talking at schools, churches, and so forth.

"Of specific practical importance to doctors is the way in which the abortion act is being implemented. This leads to a difficult ethical dilemma. The government is using the drug Misoprostol to induce abortions.

"Nurses and doctors at clinics are handing out this drug (which is actually an anti-ulcer drug and is not registered as an abortifacient) to patients. The patients are told to insert it vaginally at home. They are told to simply go to the nearest hospital once they start bleeding.

"The dilemma is that the trauma departments of hospitals are often manned by doctors and nurses with conscientious objections against performing abortions.

"Ethically, they are obliged to attend to a patient who comes in bleeding, so that they need to do the mopping up and performing the second part of the procedure (curettement or evacuation) for the abortionist. In this manner, the line between treating a complication of abortion and doing the last part of the abortion procedure is being blurred.

"This is an unacceptable state of affairs and strikes us as unethical, that the doctor who prescribes the abortifacient and then refers the patient for the mopping up procedure superimposes his ethical and moral value system on another. He also abdicates his moral and professional responsibility for the abortion that he has initiated.

"For that reason, we met with the Medical and Dental Council of South Africa. They confirmed the principle that a doctor who institutes a procedure that he or she knows will end in a surgical procedure must follow the correct referral protocol.

"Now, about the state of euthanasia in South Africa. The picture is also very bleak. The South African Law Commission has drafted a new piece of legislation on euthanasia. In this white paper, active euthanasia will be allowed:

1. when the person is clinically dead or when the patient's status is confirmed by two practitioners and cessation of treatment may take place.

2. when a competent person is terminally ill [and] requests euthanasia or assisted suicide.

3. when an incompetent, terminally ill patient [has given] advance directive power of attorney.

3. for the incompetent terminally ill patient without advance directive or power of attorney, who has either family in agreement—or the family is not willing and the patient status is confirmed by two practitioners.

"Although South Africa was in the past about twenty years behind the rest of the world, we have to a large extent caught up, and in some cases even overtaken many of the Western countries on these issues.

I want to know Christ and the power of his resurrection and the fellowship of sharing in his sufferings, becoming like him in his death, and so, somehow, to attain to the resurrection from the dead. (Philippians 3:10)

"They say that during the time of the Roman Empire, each regiment would have its own standard bearer. It was a position much sought after, even though it meant almost certain death. When they would go with a fleet to invade another country and draw near to shore, the standard bearer would be the first to jump off the ship into the shallow water. The enemy would usually be waiting for him on the beach.

"As the standard bearer jumped off the ship, he used both hands to hold the pole with the standard. The moment he landed, he would be showered with arrows and spears. Although it meant suicide to be a standard bearer, it was an honor. Especially during the time when the Roman army's morale was at its peak, soldiers would rival for the position.

"In the same way, God has called us to bear His standard. Those of us who are doctors are the first to be confronted with these issues, before the rest of the public. But to all of us as Christians, the calling comes to be in the front lines of any battle waged against the kingdom of God: to plant His standard on the

> beaches of life, even if it should mean death.
>
> "Maybe in our different countries we are the first to jump onto the beach, but what an honor! Maybe what we stand for appears foreign to most at this stage. Yet this is exactly the duty of the standard bearer—to be the first to jump onto the beach, to carry the standard high and show the way forward for others to follow."
>
> — *Albertus van Eeden, M.D.,* Doctors for Life

Assisted Suicide

Brian P. Johnston, executive director of the California Pro-Life Council, offers this assessment of the whole issue of assisted suicide:

> "Euthanasia advocates frequently assert that advances in medicine require a new ethic. Such advances, they say, suggest a need to "re-examine" how we treat those who are near the end of life.
>
> "Advances in modern medical technology supposedly call for advances in modern medical ethics. But the issue of doctors assisting in a suicide is not new.
>
> "The reality is that this is a very old issue. The difficult task of dealing with a dying patient, a patient in great pain, or the despondent and suicidal patient has

confronted the medical profession since it came into existence. Hippocrates wrote in the oath ascribed to him, " I will give no deadly medicine, even if asked."

"Hippocrates had either experienced or anticipated the pressure that would be brought to bear on physicians to use their healing knowledge to kill. Just as there are now, there were patients then who felt continued existence meant intolerable suffering, and just as now, the physician had the knowledge and the ability to kill swiftly.

"One of the host of evils that is loosed when a doctor becomes a professional killer is the very real danger of manipulated suicide. Even euthanasia advocates admit that this is a prospect that cannot be avoided. It will be nearly impossible to detect, as even the manipulator may only subconsciously 'encourage' the decision to be euthanized.

"Margaret Pabst-Battin, a long-time advocate of legalizing assisted suicide, admits that such new laws could give rise to the "large-scale manipulation of suicide, and the maneuvering of people to choose suicide when they would not otherwise have done so. This is the other, darker side of the future coin."

"Then there is something called 'infectious suicide.' One thing we know about suicide is that it can be highly contagious. The mass suicides of Jonestown and of the Heaven's

Gate cult in San Diego are only the most photographed examples.

"Much more common is the ripple effect. We are most familiar with this copycat or cluster phenomenon because of the coverage given to teen-suicide clusters. But there are much higher rates of ripple-effect suicides found in other communities. The highest rate of copycat suicide is found among older white males.

"Another dangerous phenomenon is 'spiritualized suicide.' We tend to associate suicide with the classic signs of depression. But a potential suicide may show no signs of depression. One might also assume that Christians in particular would be less inclined to accept suicide.

"Many emotionally and spiritually immature people are tempted with the notion of 'departing this veil of tears.' Often with misunderstood emotion, they will ask to employ euthanasia for a loved one. 'Can't we just let him be with God?'

"They frequently misquote Paul: 'For me to live is Christ, to die is gain' or 'I long to depart this earthly tent.' They confuse their newfound emotions for spiritual insight.

"Many Christian leaders think that in confronting euthanasia they are confronting the 'unregenerate heathen' who are imposing materialist, utilitarian values against the

> sanctity of human life. But the challenge is much greater.
>
> "Our neighbors, our friends, even those in the pew every Sunday, these are the people who are at risk in the assisted suicide debate. These "normal" people are the ones who are being targeted by the assisted suicide arguments. There is a tremendous need to equip these people with the truth.
>
> "Let's continue in the noble tradition of comforting the afflicted, not killing them; honoring the aged, and protecting the infirm.
>
> Many anthropologists, as well as Christian writers, agree that this is one of the definitions of civilization. It is perhaps our richest heritage, our finest hallmark.
>
> No, this is clearly not a new issue.
>
> —*Brian P. Johnston,* California Pro-life Council

Issues of Conscience would not be complete without a few helpful chapters on the practical aspects of modern activism. Remember, activism is just the working out of our faith in the arenas of daily life.

We learn to become more and more salty to a thirsty world looking for God. When someone is in a hot desert looking for an oasis of water, who will be there to pass the cup?

CHAPTER 14

Biblical Family Planning

Is any type of birth control method spoken of in the Bible? Can we know God's will regarding this intimate and joyous aspect of the marital relationship?

Those who seriously follow Jesus Christ want to be in God's will in all areas of life. God left no restrictions on procreation; in fact, He was highly encouraging and enthusiastic for us to "be fruitful and multiply."

In the New Covenant, the marriage bed is spoken of as "pure and undefiled." That pretty much means almost anything is allowable in the conjugal joy of a couple. And a natural outcome of sexual intercourse is the creation of a child having its parental characteristics.

Are we to be responsible for His great gift of having children? You bet.

How is God glorified in our family planning?

One authority in the area of birth control methods is a medical doctor and great pro-life crusader, John C. Willke, the president of the International Right to Life Federation. I once shared a train ride with him and his wife, Barbara, into Amsterdam one very frigid December morning. Both told me of their burning vision to educate and train people in pro-life issues.

The following article was written by Dr. Willke for his newsletter. It gives the correct definitions for many medical terms we need to understand. A very sharp tool of the enemy is to keep us confused with verbiage; we must clear it up so we may take godly instruction.

Emergency Contraception

Conception, fertilization, implantation, a human life—all can be confusing terms. Human life, biologically speaking, begins at the first cell stage. This has been a known scientific fact for more than a hundred years. Fertilization or the "moment of conception" is the union of sperm and egg.

There has been considerable misunderstanding regarding emergency contraception. First, here are some proven medical facts: Sperm deposited in a woman's body can reach her ovaries in as little as thirty minutes. If an ovum "awaits," fertilization (conception) can occur at that time.

After fertilization/conception, this single cell contains within it a totally new male or female human. Nothing will be added to this new human from this time until he or she dies, nothing except nutrition and oxygen.

For the next seven days, this new human embryo floats freely down the woman's fallopian tube and will then implant itself into the nutrient lining of her womb. In a few days, he or she taps into the mother's bloodstream and sends a chemical-hormonal message into her blood. This is carried to a gland at the base of her brain. Through this mechanism, this new passenger stops the mother's menstrual period.

On the day her menses is due yet does not occur, it has been one month since the onset of her last menstrual period, two weeks since fertilization, and one week since implantation. When the mother is four to six days late for her period, the fetal heart of the new human being within her begins to beat.

The word conception is used in two ways. The traditional meaning has been union of sperm and ovum as in fertilization. The new usage of this term has redefined it to mean the time of implantation. When used in this way, contraceptives include pills, IUDs, and "emergency contraception."

The word 'pregnancy' has also been used recently by some with a new meaning. Traditionally, it has always been defined as beginning at fertilization/conception. A newer usage defines pregnancy as beginning

> when the woman's body is affected by the attachment of the new embryo, at implantation.
>
> When using conception and pregnancy in these newly defined meanings, honesty requires that the user specifically state his or her meaning to be at the implantation rather than the traditional meaning, which the overwhelming majority of listeners hear it to be.
>
> The term emergency contraception is very misleading. In view of the thirty-minute transit time of sperm, if an ovum "awaits," fertilization occurs and a new human life begins. The woman then is pregnant before she gets out of bed. The use of pills twelve to twenty-four hours later *cannot possibly prevent* human life from beginning.
>
> But these pills also have the effect of hardening the lining of the womb. Then, when this one-week-old human reaches the womb, he or she cannot implant and dies. This is an abortion. Emergency contraception, when it "works," is not contraception. It is an abortifacient.
>
> *—Dr. John C. Willke*

What Are Abortifacients?

While we are touching on this subject of abortifacients, it might be helpful to see something from another pro-life activist, Roger Domingo, taken from his book, *Orphans in Babylon*, nine years in the making. It's an extraordinary volume geared to giving answers to the pressing questions that the opposition raises. This particular subject sheds light on an area that many pro-life couples have regarding the taking of birth control medications: Do they really cause the abortion of tiny fetuses—or do they prevent the sperm from reaching the egg so that conception never occurs?

> "The surgical abortion holocaust involves the conscious complicity of mothers in the deaths of 1.5 million American babies per year. Some of the figures indicate that abortifacient birth control methods [IUDs, Norplant, Depo-Provera, The Pill], may kill eight million to twelve million tiny babies every year, a holocaust five to eight times as great as surgical abortion.
>
> "Add that together, and we get almost fourteen million deaths."

These figures are consistent with those offered by pro-life activist Brian Clowes: "Some researchers (using very conservative figures) have calculated that the birth control pill directly causes between 1.53 and 4.15 million chemical abortions per year. This means between one to two and a half times the total number of surgical abortions committed in this country every year!"

Why have churches and, indeed, the pro-life movement, concentrated its focus almost exclusively on surgical abortion while chemical abortion has been a massacre of greater magnitude?

Because of relativism, emotion, and ignorance, perhaps. How many Christians know that their method of birth control is what kills their newly conceived babies?

In 1990, Professor Janet Smith wrote in *When Choice Becomes God:* "Increasing numbers of women [were] beginning to realize that certain forms of contraceptives—including the IUD or coil, [then] largely in disuse because of adverse side-effects and the so-called 'morning-after' pill—are in fact abortifacients. No mention was made of the abortifacient nature of The Pill in general use."

Smith's conclusions are piercing, since many Christians who value life and understand the very nature of God as the way, the truth, and the life have never been informed that the birth control methods they might be using are, indeed, abortifacients causing the demise of the tiny-celled fetus.

There is confusion, perhaps, because preventing conception (the union of sperm with egg) can be accomplished by other methods such as condoms and vaginal shields, which are designed to prevent sperm from ever reaching the egg.

But no method, except abstinence, is 100 percent fail-safe.

"Contraception facilitates the kind of relationships and even the kind of attitudes and moral character that are likely to lead to abortion. The contraceptive mentality treats sexual intercourse as though it had little natural connection with babies; it thinks of babies as an 'accident' of intercourse, as an unwelcome intrusion into a sexual relationship, as a burden," Smith writes.

It does not matter by what method a child is conceived. Every baby conceived is God's blessing to the family and to the world.

Others, like Mercedes Arzú Wilson and many Roman Catholics, advocate the natural birth control method, whereby couples choose to not join sexually during charted fertile times of the monthly cycle. This method certainly takes the most loving self-control and seems to be the most guilt-free.

A Birth Control Holocaust

We asked the American Life League: "Is there a medical connection between birth control and abortion? There seems to be quite a discussion, as even married couples want to follow God in a holy manner." Following is their response:

> Birth control is society's answer to the rise in unwanted pregnancies. Many say abortions will decrease as better birth control methods hit the market. Can The Pill, Norplant, RU-486, Depo-Provera and "emergency contraception" decrease the rate of abortion? Not likely.
>
> One of the ways that these chemicals and devices work is by preventing the fertilized egg from attaching to the lining of the uterus. Conception (fertilization) has occurred.

A new tiny person has been formed and is traveling on his or her way down the fallopian tube to enter the womb, where he or she will grow until birth.

If the fertilized egg cannot attach to the uterus (womb), the baby dies. Most of the time, the mother and father are totally unaware that the woman was pregnant. Birth control has turned babies into disposable objects.

Pregnancy is no longer seen as a blessing but a curse. Parents of large families are looked down upon, instead of held in high esteem. We now place more value on getting big salaries, driving nice cars, and living in huge homes.

Young married couples want to wait years before starting families, because they have learned from our society that children will take away their freedom. So if a child is not "planned," abortion becomes a likely option for the couple who cannot view that child as a great blessing.

We need to remember that the only plans we should be making are plans to live out God's will—not our will. We need to give our families and ourselves fully to Him, and let Him take care of the schedule of events. God creates babies, and He has a plan for every one of them.

Only when we can see babies, children, and all people as part of God's plan will abortion truly decrease. Birth control is not the solution. It's part of the problem.

The Family-Centered Approach

Mercedes Arzú Wilson once sent me several copies of her book *Love and Family: Raising a Traditional Family in a Secular World.* It's a comprehensive resource guide written by a parent for parents and for educators who work with children. It includes the experiences of some outstanding leaders in the scientific, social and religious sectors.

Mercedes' family-centered approach, with extensive references and suggestions, empowers parents who wish to reclaim their position as the primary educators of their children, especially in the field of sexuality.

I've chosen one section that is usually not addressed: "Abortion on Demand: The Supply of Human Flesh for Fetal Tissue Research." As gruesome as that may sound, some members of the scientific community are eager to profit by the deaths of unborn babies.

Just the possibility (and it is a strong one) of a growing scientific trend toward using living tissues is horrifying. The thought of that should double our efforts to educate people to either produce children or abstain from sexual relations so as not to produce children.

We can only do this by God's guidance and grace. Toward this end, Mercedes offers solutions that can stop the killing—through massive education and other non-destructive means. She comments: "In one of his first official actions in 1992, U.S. President Clinton lifted the federal government's existing ban against scientific research using tissues obtained from babies killed by induced abortion. Such research has been fueled by claims that injecting fetal cells into the brains of persons suffering from Parkinson's disease has helped to alleviate patients' symptoms."

According to a letter written by Professor Linda Gourash, M.D.:

> *"The 1989 Archives of Neurology* published the most detailed description of this procedure, outlining that an unborn baby's brain must be selectively sucked out by a tube inserted in the mother's womb to ensure that the living fetal brain cells are harvested in fresh transplantable condition. This process *kills the fetus,* who is then aborted."

News from Edinburgh, Scotland, tells us that researchers are working to perfect a process whereby eggs from aborted baby girls could be implanted into living women in order to help them achieve a pregnancy. In an editorial for *The Catholic World Report* on this subject, Philip F. Lawler writes:

> "Having severed the link between the process of reproduction and the act of marital love, the researchers are now laboriously trying to patch together their own artificial sequence

> of causes and effects. And like simple children with a complicated jigsaw puzzle, they can't fit the pieces together properly."

My thought on that is that medicine is being prostituted to cannibalize the young for the benefit of the old.

During the past decade, scientists have made enormous strides in understanding the process of human reproduction, yet the incidence of sterility has reached unprecedented levels. From their earliest days of school, youngsters are taught how to avoid sexually transmitted diseases, yet epidemics of those diseases are ripping through our society.

Pharmacists offer a bewildering array of devices to thwart the process of conception, yet "unplanned" pregnancies are soaring out of control. And now the good doctors of Edinburgh offer the ghoulish promise that "while we butcher unborn children in the womb, we might yet raise up healthy lives from their dismembered corpses."

Presumably, as with other fetal tissue uses, these tiny egg cells would have to be harvested while the soon-to-be-aborted baby is still alive. Philip Lawler continues:

> "For millennia, the process of pregnancy was expected to flow naturally out of an act of love. And lo and behold, that natural system usually worked without flaw, without any wizard's intervention. Oh, there have always

> been those who sought to thwart that process; the 'magicians' were at work even in the days of ancient Israel. But until this brave new century, their enterprises were generally recognized as perversions.
>
> "Through all those millennia, a young woman knew that she could bear a child if she made one loving act of self-giving. For fashionable women today, pregnancy involves two more careful calculations: the decision to eschew contraceptives, then the decision to forego an abortion. And for increasing numbers of women—thanks to modern science—pregnancy can occur without that self-surrender. A child born today has no guarantee that his life began with an act of love.
>
> "If life is a gift, how can we snatch it away from the baby girl who was aborted to start this whole process? If every birth in effect justifies itself, should we churn out as many children as possible, by every means at our disposal, fair or foul? And if an act can be justified simply because it brings happiness to someone, are any moral restraints intact?"

As another observer puts it, "Common sense tells us that dead tissue is not useful for human transplantation. Have you ever heard of someone getting a kidney or other organ that was transplanted from a cadaver? No, tissue for transplantation must be living...Doctors must extract living tissue, which, consequently, tortures and kills the [unborn] child."

How could any scientist rationalize such macabre acts? Incredibly, some try. "Abortion is a tragedy," says one transplant researcher. "But as long as it occurs, I believe it is immoral to let tissues and materials go to waste."

Surprisingly, a self-proclaimed "pro-choice feminist," professor Janice Raymond of the University of Massachusetts and MIT, was among those who echoed the warning. "Fetal transplants would increase abortions, and make women mere factories for medical experiments. Women become the resources whose bodies are mined for scientific gold."

Mercedes Wilson gives us this last challenge: "The future of humanity is in our hands. We must rescue the family from the claws of darkness. As we enter the third millennium, we must unite with those who are sincerely concerned about the future of mankind. Our influence as parents and educators can defeat the forces of darkness.

"We must not underestimate the power of self-control that young people possess and should be challenged to put into practice. 'True love waits for marriage' is the answer to their future happiness. And married couples do not have to remain slaves to the lucrative market of artificial birth control, abortion, or sterilization that continues to exploit them.

"Natural family planning unites the couple, increases communication, and contributes to the disappearance of divorce."

Are you looking for some strategies for life that will put together your thinking on these issues of conscience? It is good to take time to meditate on the words of Scripture in light of preserving life in the culture of death that embraces the world right now.

Wouldn't it be wonderful to go back to the innocent age of the 1890s or 1950s when legalities were followed simply and medical practice was always a life of service, with one proposition—that of saving the patient?

Oh, well.

Let's get on to the strategy part, because life is serious—and we are in just one small battle in the scope of global warfare for souls. That is where we are going next—to the enclaves of the war room.

Section V

Strategies For Life

CHAPTER 15

Methods for Activism

There are many ways to become active in this fight for life. We hope that after reading the cries of those who have contributed to the making of this book by living it out, you will be informed and stirred in your spirit to begin your own God-called activism.

As you have seen, many have purposed to stand with God in the kingdom fight for life. That is our final battle.

The fight for life—to allow it, to preserve it, to evangelize the lost, to heal the sick, bring justice to the needy, clothe the naked, feed the hungry, deliver from demons, and make strong disciples for this battle—this is the mandate of Christ's kingdom.

This section will provide examples of what Christians have done and are doing as activists for life. The action may be as simple as writing e-mails to your political leaders or as self-sacrificing as going to China and standing in Tiananmen Square. You might be called upon to dedicate yourself to intercessory prayer warfare or become an errand-runner for life issues activists at U.N. conferences.

Others have served by editing or translating the life message into other languages so as to reach other nations. Some go from sidewalk referral counseling outside abortion centers, to drafting law, volunteering help in crises, giving food, finances, wisdom, and a temporary home for the abused.

It can be anything at all, because the Holy Spirit equips us differently so we can be effectively incorporated into the battle.

What a privilege! Look for your place!

What good is it, my brothers, if a man claims to have faith but has no deeds? Can such faith save him? In the same way, faith by itself, if it is not accompanied by action, is dead. (James 2:14, 17)

Children of the Millennium

Following is part of a letter written by our friend Drs. Dorenbos to Richard Holbrook, U.S. ambassador to the United Nations. Copies of the letter were also distributed at an international conference on "The Children of the New Millennium," held in November 1999 in The Hague.

> "What about our children in the new millennium? How can we lead our children into the new

millennium if we know that millions and millions of the world's current children are in forced slavery, more than the number of all the slaves of our past combined?

"How dare we allow just one more day to pass in which children are forced into prostitution that one million helpless children or more suffer each year?

"What can we say about the dying children, especially the girl-child of the Far East and India who are cowardly killed through United Nations-sponsored programs like UNICEF, International Planned Parenthood (which the West funds), the International Monetary Fund, and The World Bank?

"These succeed in educating women to get abortions, become sterilized without their informed consent, commit infanticide at the medical level, and abandon especially the girl-child to open annihilation and continued persecution.

"The population controllers are more geared to increasing the abortion rate than to protecting the lives of all newborn babies. Did you know that more babies are killed by abortion every year than there were victims in World War II? That is about fifty-five million each year!

"That is why we implore you to reshuffle the global structure of U.N. institutions that focus on birth control methods while denying much needed antibiotics and clean water sources. We

> urge you to not hesitate to strongly protest and halt the abuse of children, their untimely deaths and impending disasters that the children of this new decade, this next millennium, are facing very seriously.
>
> "If you and we are too slow and hesitate too long to end these present and clear dangers, we will never pass on the legacy of providing a 'safe place to live' for all our world's children. You must speak for those with no voice.
>
> "It is our longing to work toward this end as long as the Lord God is waiting to see what the men and women placed in strategic, global-changing positions are willing to do with the authority He has given them. This is very grave in your particular situation. *Please take this to heart.*"
>
> *—Dr. Bert P. Dorenbos, president, Cry for Life board member, The International Right to Life Federation*

The Coming Collision

The following e-mail demonstrates yet another method of activism: research and dissemination of information on global problems. Dr. Hirsen, an attorney and radio host over the Internet's American Freedom Network, uses the airwaves as a forum of interchange among all kinds of listeners.

You, too, can call radio shows to give pro-life comments, correct misinformation, provide fresh, vibrant news, and field questions that anyone on any level can understand. These methods demonstrate doable activism for life concerns, right from your home telephone!

> "We have some very important obligations to which we must attend to in the process of living our lives in a righteous manner.
>
> *"First of all, we are to be good stewards of the bounty that has been so generously bestowed upon us.*
>
> " Our founding documents, the Declaration of Independence and The Constitution, demonstrate unprecedented inspiration that was providentially directed. The way our government has been formulated, we have neither monarchs nor kings, but instead, our political leaders are our employees...We must not allow ambivalence, lethargy, or piety to hinder us from engaging in the vital duty of patriotic custodianship.
>
> *"Second, we must remain eternally optimistic.*
>
> "The faithful have sometimes been confused by the teaching to be *in* the world but not *of* the world. Some people have interpreted this to mean that the kingdom must be outside of the existing world, or a dominion that is to come in the future, rather than one that exists now...The loser in such an equation is society as a whole. The lack of contribution from those who are morally minded results in a cultural

decline by default, as the population suffers from the lack of ethical input.

"On the other hand, when spiritual actuality is viewed as inseparable from the world, it acknowledges the wholeness and integrity of creation. With this hallowed perspective, we can fulfill our responsibilities and permit ourselves to be instruments in effecting positive change.

"Third, we must be wise and skillful in our approach.

"Responsible citizenship takes courage. Cynicism and disillusionment are dangerous and contagious maladies that induce otherwise virtuous people to retreat from their civic and moral obligations.

"The freedom to be born, to live, to raise and educate our children, to worship, and to own private property are sacred rights.

"Aleksandr Solzhenitsyn, who stared into the face of totalitarianism in the Soviet Union, spoke of the loss of freedoms in the Western world when he said, 'Tragically, however, the free West will only believe it when it is no longer free. To quote a Russian proverb, "'When it happens you will know it is true, but then it is too late.'"

"There is a battle taking place between good and evil. For good to triumph, the adversary must be fully examined and confronted. Our battlefields lie within societal institutions, cultural mores, and political operations. We must employ intelligent strategies, as well as prudent restraint when necessary, in our efforts.

"Fourth, we must be the salt and light.

"To obey this mandate, responsible citizens must write, speak, defend, protest, legislate, and otherwise engage the culture. When we withdraw into a protected cocoon, we concede the rudder of society to the moral relativists. As C.S. Lewis so aptly said, 'We cannot remain silent and concede everything away.'

"Without fully partaking in our governmental processes, costly liberties that enable Americans to pursue meaningful lives are jeopardized.

"Freedom is not self-sustaining. Rather, it is something that must be forever cultivated and safeguarded. At the very least, this means being informed, casting votes in an election (and) bravely taking a public stand to defend and protect our rights.

"In addition, we must also try to recover ground that has been lost.

"The symptoms of a society that suffers from a deficiency of scruples are prominently and painfully displayed to the dismay of self-appointed experts. Divorce, abortion, crime, pornography, substance abuse, and corruption at the highest levels of national and international government are lamentable signs of the times.

"However, it is here that we can become that substance that preserves life (salt) in a dying world. We can shine as beacons, to light the way for a lost people.

"Lastly, we cannot stand idly by and watch the plans of internationalists collide with individual freedoms. Thousands of years ago, the ancient Hebrew prophet Isaiah warned Israel of a future time where some would call evil good and good evil. We witness this type of moral confusion occurring in all strata of our culture, but as we have seen, this is particularly true at the international level.

"The intimate decisions involving our families and our private pursuits must be protected from international influence. The definitions of marriage, family, and parenting must be preserved in their original, divinely inspired statuses. We must defend liberty and preserve our nation for the sake of our forefathers and the future of our children's children.

"Most of all, in everything, we must pray as our founding fathers did. When our people rely upon His providence once again, He will preserve and revive our nation."

—Dr. James Hirsen

Media Infiltration

Following on the heels of Dr. Hirsen's comments is a reminder of another powerful action avenue: media infiltration. Recently, Christians got together to apply to a charitable trust for funds to educate reporters from the largest communications networks by spending a day and a half listening to theologians and academic experts.

How better to teach them who we are, what our principles are, and what life issues matter to us than to spend time on revealing and hopefully correcting the anti-religious bias so prevalent in liberal media circles?

Among those who signed up for the event were journalists from ABC's *Nightline, CNN, The Wall Street Journal* and the *Los Angeles Times.* The seminars were conducted by the Ethics and Public Policy Center, a Washington, D.C.-based group that received a $925,000 grant from the Pew Charitable Trusts to bring the discussion of religion to the media representatives. The event included seminars and luncheons, a content analysis of thirty years of media coverage of religion, and three summit meetings.

Dr. Death

Another effective life strategy is to put grassroots pressure on our legislative bodies to chip away at pro-death laws that have been passed and to construct new laws that enhance and allow for life options.

What our legislators often lack is the will of the people. In countries around the world that allow for public input, the support of pro-life candidates and office holders is crucial. They may not be able to get the full extent of pro-life law implemented, but with patience, little by little, progress for life is possible.

We must work for any size dent in the pro-death movement's victories, even if they are not all we want at the present. Start with banning partial-birth abortion first, and then work on other parts of abortion until its legality is overturned.

Drs. Dorenbos received the following letter from a pro-life legislator in Michigan. This has been the infamous hotbed of physician-assisted suicide fanatically led by "Dr. Death," Jack Kevorkian, who has admitted to "assisting" in more than 130 deaths.

This pro-life history is told by assistant majority floor leader William Van Regenmorter, who wrote a comprehensive letter explaining what he has done (and what can be done) in the legislative process. Oh, that we had hundreds more like him! He truly cares for and guards both tiny and elderly citizens who have no voice.

> "In Michigan, Jack Kevorkian, a disbarred pathologist, has admitted to participating in more than 130 deaths. While information about many of those deaths has not been revealed by Kevorkian, the medical examiner for the county in which most of the deaths have occurred indicated many were suspicious and, in all likelihood, homicides.
>
> "Kevorkian was tried in court three times for assisted suicide, twice under common law and once under a long-since repealed, badly flawed statute. He was acquitted in each of them, but significant questions have been asked about that process. For example, jurors

indicated confusion about elements of assisted suicide, and two of the judges were appealed successfully during the trial, more than twelve times. In contrast, the ten-month O. J. Simpson murder trial, with dozens of lawyers representing each side, resulted in only one appeal.

"It was clear Michigan needed a statute that set forth the elements of assisted suicide with clarity and concision. As that proposal was making its way through the legislature, a group called Merian's Friends, which had formed to support Jack Kevorkian, spent nearly seven hundred thousand dollars to pay petition circulators to gather signatures, successfully placing the issue before the Michigan voters [as Proposal B].

"In the meantime, Senate Bill 200 (the ban) passed the legislature with strong bipartisan support and went into effect September 1, 1998. However, the pending public vote on Proposal B was scheduled for November 3, and had that been successful, the statutory ban would have been superseded.

"Recognizing the dangers of legalizing assisted suicide and the slippery slope which would have inevitably followed, the people of Michigan overwhelmingly defeated Proposal B, and the statute outlawing assisted suicide is now in effect.

"Challenging that statute, Kevorkian put a person to death while videotaping the process and later participated in a national television program on which the tape was presented.

> "The prosecutor has charged Kevorkian with premeditated murder, as well as under the new assisted suicide law. In Michigan courts, the jury may have a choice of convicting on all charges or certain charges, but it is clear that in addition to the November 3 rejection of assisted suicide, this will be a defining moment for the state.
>
> "You have my strongest support for the important work you are trying to accomplish."
>
> —*William Van Regenmorter, Michigan State Senator*

Several things may be recognized and learned as strategy in Senator Van Regenmorter's letter. Kevorkian, as a rabid activist for his belief in assisting the physically incapacitated to end their lives, acts on those beliefs through access to whatever legal death-dealing agents he can procure.

He has assistants and a support group, which joined the battle by going to voters and getting a petition signed in order to have it presented to the Michigan legislature. So pro-death advocates use the "grassroots pressure" technique, too.

At that point, it would be up to the Michigan House and Senate to come to a common agreement on which way to go with formulating their bill. Should they believe a handful of pro-death people pushing for physician-assisted suicide that flies in the face of years of American medical tradition and justice for all? Or advance a sweeping bill to make sure *no law* is possible that would allow any physician to assist in the suicide of another human?

This had far-reaching ramifications. Would letters, e-mails, and calls come in from the community to help cement their convictions to preserve life?

Time is *always* of the essence.

People had to act and did, passing the ban in September 1998, two months before a public vote could take place. That is why timely phone calls, letters, e-mails, community awareness campaigns, and demonstrations assist legislators in determining the "will of the people" that they are obligated to fulfill. Studies show that one telephone call or contact with a legislator represents twenty-five thousand citizens. Look at the power of one contact!

Next, we have an update from Dr. John C. Willke on what took place a few months after the Michigan legislation was passed:

A God-Defying Act

"A Michigan court has sentenced Jack Kevorkian to ten to twenty-five years in prison for killing a man on *60 Minutes*. He was also given three to seven years for delivery of a controlled substance. The judge, Jessica Cooper, stated the following at that time:

> ...(I)t was about lawlessness. It was about disrespect for a society that exists because of the strength of the legal system.
>
> No one, sir, is above the law. No one. You had the audacity to go on national television,

show the world what you did, and dare the legal system to stop you. Well, sir, consider yourself stopped. The American public clearly rejects killing as a way of solving medical problems.

In fact, the most lopsided vote ever recorded on the question of assisted suicide occurred right here in Michigan last fall, with the defeat of Proposal B, by a vote of 71 to 29. With this vote, the citizens of Michigan reassured the nation of their sound judgment in rejecting killing as a response to disease or disability. Those of goodwill should now unite to provide care of our sick; getting existing pain relief techniques to patients in discomfort; screening and treating for depression and demoralization among those fighting disease; and supporting hospice care for the families of those who need it.

"I watched part of that trial by cable television and saw the slumped shoulders of an old man—Kevorkian—with grizzled head bent, still fighting for his perceived 'right' to be a medical serial killer above the law. Some of those he helped to take their lives demonstrated no disease at all upon autopsy. A few other of his assisted deaths were brought into question when a spouse heavily insisted on the 'assistance.'

"Other autopsies revealed people Kevorkian 'assisted' with curable diseases, who, with compassionate and responsible pain relief provided, could have lived much longer. But it was most interesting to hear Kevorkian (in his 70s) state after he lost his case and would most assuredly spend all his remaining days in prison, that he would commit suicide, because 'prison was too dire to endure.' To this date, he has either not succeeded or not tried to end his own life.

"Suicide is actually a supremely self-centered, God-defying act. There may be many excuses to come up with to decide for suicide or euthanasia. Certainly, every medical avenue should be traveled to relieve unbearable pain. However, the moment of death is God-ordained, not man-ordained.

"Suicide is demonically inspired. When humans are at their lowest point, that is most often the very place when God is called upon to step in. How many stories have we heard from those who unsuccessfully attempted suicide and later were grateful to their 'rescuers' who prevented their moment of death so they could step back, find alternatives, and embrace life again.

"Never give up.

"Never give in.

"Seek God and get help.

—Dr. John C. Willke

My frame was not hidden from you when I was made in the secret place. When I was woven together in the depths of the earth, your eyes saw my unformed body. All the days ordained for me were written in your book before one of them came to be. (Psalm 139:15-16)

How to Become an Activist

Network with pro-life leaders; become a leader

Collect pro-life e-mail addresses

Assemble government agencies' e-mails for mailing campaigns

Use the Internet for spreading the pro-life message

Form and join pro-life prayer enclaves

Educate and support your clergy in life issues activism

Donate, volunteer, host, organize, make calls, go to conferences

Petition for justice and non-lethal health care

Study and know the truth about the sanctity of human life

A Prayer for This Age

Heavenly Father, we come before You today to ask Your forgiveness and to seek Your direction and guidance. We know Your Word says, "Woe on those who call evil good," but that's exactly what we have done.

We have lost our spiritual equilibrium and reversed our values.

We confess that:

We have ridiculed the absolute truth of Your Word and called it *pluralism.*

We have worshiped other gods and called it *multiculturalism.*

We have endorsed perversion and called it an *alternative lifestyle.*

We have exploited the poor and called it the *lottery.*

We have neglected the needy and called it *self-preservation.*

We have rewarded laziness and called it *welfare.*

We have killed our unborn children and called it *a choice.*

We have shot abortionists and called it *justifiable.*

We have neglected to discipline our children and called it *building self-esteem.*

We have abused power and called it *political savvy.*

We have coveted our neighbors' possessions and called it *ambition.*

We have polluted the air with profanity and pornography and called it *freedom of expression.*

We have ridiculed the time-honored values of our forefathers and called it *enlightenment.*

Search us, O God, and know our hearts today; cleanse us from every sin and set us free. Guide and bless the men and women who have been sent to direct us to the center of Your will.

We ask it in the name of Your Son, the living Savior, Jesus Christ.

Amen.

—From J.I.A.L. Ministries

CHAPTER 16

Activism Around the Globe

On the international front is a Catholic family agency that serves as a watchdog in law, medical trends, human rights violations, and the vagaries of the United Nations' every move. Headed by Austin Ruse, the Catholic Family & Human Rights Institute has an impressive legal awareness team that has watched over the abortion issue and the euthanasia movement in various parts of the globe.

I was present at one such meeting with other denominations who were striving to do whatever was necessary—from grassroots activism to legislative lobbying—in an attempt to stop an Oregon euthanasia initiative. They were present as "friends of the court" in the *Vacco v. Quill* U.S. Supreme Court case regarding legalized euthanasia. Our side prevailed—this time.

First, here's a letter I sent to Chief Justice William Rehnquist regarding this issue:

Dear Sir:

I am compelled to write to you as a citizen of this great nation before your final consideration of *Vacco v. Quill* regarding the possible introduction of physician-assisted suicide into our land...

I implore you, along with the Associate Justices, to deeply consider retaining homicide as a crime. The direct purpose of our Constitution was framed to preserve and recognize life in ways that benefit the general welfare of the entire Union. That means no malicious discrimination against *any* of its citizens, no matter how helpless, voiceless, impaired, terminally ill, demented, or elderly. A wise conclusion will reach broadly above and beyond the clamor of a minority who, for purely individualistic reasons, would selfishly tear the fabric of a united people which has by its Constitution, natural law, general assent, and traditions given herself to the preservation of the value of all human life.

In this, you stand more powerful than the president and a Congress divided against itself, and therefore, against the people whom they represent, because your decision will ensure the chance of life to future generations of Americans...the Supreme Court's interpretation regarding *Vacco v. Quill* will define Constitutional truth regarding our

> general welfare. I join the majority of Americans to plead that you not go against the spirit of our Constitution and the Bill of Rights to limit the freedom of simply being alive. Doing otherwise will be immeasurably destructive. Physician-assisted euthanasia would irreparably scar and divide this nation, just as abortion on demand has done.
>
> What a tremendous responsibility and accounting every one of you have before the God of Life, the Providence of our great nation! This is what I ask: Where will the killing stop? Will it stop with you, before it is judiciously sanctioned?
>
> *—In God we trust, Laurel T. Hughes, Ph.D.*

Some time ago, I received an e-mail from Ruse that describes another method of pulling grassroots people together, by educating and supplying information on how to make a difference. A Web site was created as a clearinghouse for this one issue. Anyone could do the same.

A Call From the Families of the World

Ruse was among the twenty-six men and women who met in Rome in 1998 to draft a document titled "A Call From the Families of the World." Participants were Roman Catholic, evangelicals and mainline Protestants, Latter-day Saints, Eastern Orthodox, Jewish, and Sunni and Shiite Muslims. The one-page statement, to be signed by a goal of two million people, was to be presented to the United Nations in the spring of 2000.

It affirmed that "The natural family is the fundamental social unit, inscribed in human nature, and centered around the voluntary union of a man and a woman in a lifelong covenant of marriage." The Call stated that the purpose of the family is:

* to satisfy the longings of the human heart to give and receive love,
* to welcome and ensure the full physical and emotional development of children,
* to share a home that serves as the center for social, educational, economic, and spiritual life,
* to build strong bonds among the generations to pass on a way of life that has transcendent meaning,
* to extend a hand of compassion to individuals and households whose circumstances fall short of these ideals.

To make this accessible to millions, Ruse created an online copy of the document that could be signed by visitors to his Web site. He urged online visitors to print out The Call and send copies to their friends; send it electronically to everyone in the visitor's e-mail address book; place printouts in churches and synagogues; and start a local project with a goal of a thousand signatures from the visitor's community.

This is the kind of grassroots project that does not require a great expenditure of money or travel time.

Great Britain

Crossing the Atlantic to the British Isles, we pinpoint a valiant, groundbreaking group founded and led by Phyllis Bowman, an indomitable woman who has stood for life for decades. She founded SPUC, The Society for the Protection of Unborn Children. It stands as a beacon to the rest of the world.

Their educational arm, British Victims of Abortion (BVA), was set up in 1987 by the SPUC Educational Research Trust. This was created in response to the many women who suffered emotional difficulties following an abortion that severely affected their quality of life—now most commonly known as Post-Abortion Syndrome (PAS).

I recently read their book, *And Still They Weep,* and it profoundly affected me, bringing stinging tears of compassion and an immensely deeper understanding into what women who have chosen abortion have to face.

The following contribution is an excerpt from a SPUC-produced treatise on activism at the parliamentarian level and on a proposal to liberalize the nation's abortion law.

> The government is obviously determined to impose changes in the abortion law that defies public opinion and would increase the number of abortions. Public opinion is opposed to further liberalization of the abortion law. In last October's Gallup poll, only 26 percent

of respondents supported abortion on demand, and only 17 percent supported changing the law to make abortion easier to obtain.

In fact, 41 percent said abortion should be made more difficult to obtain.

"Chris" had a second-trimester abortion. The next morning, intravenous antibiotics were administered because the abortionist suspected that she may have sustained a uterine perforation. She later required a hysterectomy. At that time, her pelvic cavity contained bloody, foul-smelling fluid and her uterus was necrotic. Cultures...revealed gas gangrene, a fermentative bacteria commonly found in soil, feces, and sewage. Eventually she had to be put on dialysis. —Mark Crutcher, Lime 5

The government's attempt to extend the abortion law has the ultimate objective of imposing it on Northern Ireland, despite the opposition of the majority of people there to any weakening of their legislation on abortion.

No one should be misled by claims that to make abortion more easily available will reduce the number of late abortions. Since abortion up to birth on some grounds became legal in 1991, the number of very late abortions has increased fourfold. There is no suggestion that the government wants to tighten the law to stop late abortions. Until they do, they should not expect their current claims be taken seriously.

If the Abortion Act, which was supposed to legalize abortion in rare medical cases, has led to abortion virtually on demand giving society a "license to pressurize" expectant mothers, consider how much worse such pressures would become under a law explicitly permitting abortion on demand or encouraging more readily available abortion.

There is a grave danger that such legislation would, for the first time in British legal history, create a "right" for a mother to have her unborn baby killed.

As former mass abortionist Dr. Bernard Nathanson has observed: "What is surprising is that the Stone Age thinking—the division of pregnancy into the trimesters, wherein the first trimester connotes no human presence and the second trimester does—still pervades thinking in the abortion arena."

The mounting evidence of a link between induced abortion and breast cancer challenges the suggestion that first trimester abortion is less dangerous to the mother in the long-term than later procedures.

The authors of the most comprehensive analysis of published studies found "no reason to suspect that generally earlier terminations would not also be associated with increased breast cancer risk."

Among women who developed breast cancer while pregnant, those who carried pregnancy to term had a 20 percent survival rate; those who miscarried received more aggressive treatment and had a 42 percent survival rate; but every woman who chose abortion died. —R.M. Clark & T. Chua, Clinical Oncology, Royal College of Radiologists

---

Dr. Joel Brind has since pointed out in a critique of a Danish study that despite the authors' conclusion that "induced abortions have no overall effect on the risk of breast cancer," the data from this study actually reveals a significantly increased risk associated with second trimester abortion.

However, even if future studies confirm this, the fact remains that those who assert the "safety" of abortion in the first trimester are typically referring to immediate complications and ignore the evidence of the increased risk of developing breast cancer.

French legislation of 1975 explicitly allows abortion for social reasons up to ten weeks (but up to birth for eugenic and "grave health" reasons). For most of the period between 1976 and 1988 (for which records are available), French abortion rates were higher

> than those in the UK—in addition to which there is the problem of under-reporting in France and the proportion of French women who have abortions in other countries, including England.
>
> While the pro-death activists sit in their ivory towers and coldly discuss the statistics of abortion, the abortionists pull those statistics out of women's bodies, one tragedy at a time.

Northern Ireland

Northern Irish law protects unborn children. The law on abortion in Northern Ireland is virtually identical to the legislation in England and Wales before the 1967 Abortion Act. These statutes prohibit abortion, establishing no exceptions other than acts to "preserve the life of the mother."

Northern Irish courts have allowed abortions in a few cases. However, this case law makes it clear that abortion on demand is not lawful in Northern Ireland.

Even in the landmark English case *R. V. Bourne* (1939), which resulted in the acquittal of the doctor responsible for the abortion, the judge stated: "The protection that the law gives to human life extends also to the unborn child in the womb [who] must not be destroyed unless the destruction of that child is for the purpose of preserving the yet more precious life of the mother."

In the most recent abortion case in Northern Ireland, the judge held that the mother's life "meant something more than physical or mental health such as happiness...[rather it meant that] the adverse effect must be permanent or long term and cannot be short term...a real and serious adverse effect which was sufficiently grave to warrant termination."

The people of Northern Ireland had, through every democratic means, expressed their overwhelming opposition to any liberalization of their abortion legislation.

Virginia Bottomley, Health Minister at the time, said in debate in 1990: "To the best of my knowledge, no Northern Ireland Member of Parliament has ever called for changes in the Northern Ireland abortion laws. Similarly, all the soundings of opinion have made it very clear that there is no will in Northern Ireland for such a change."

Two thirds of doctors responding to the most extensive survey of Northern Irish medical opinion on abortion opposed the extension of the Abortion Act. The survey was conducted in 1987 by Belfast-based Dr. Sean Ferguson, who wrote to 2,585 doctors and got replies from 1,575. Even a seriously flawed public opinion poll in Northern Ireland recently promoted by pro-abortionists showed only a minority in favor of abortion on social grounds.

In this 1994 poll, carried out by Ulster Marketing Surveys Limited (which was flawed in that it excluded people older than 45), of those questioned only 30 percent agreed with abortion "where the woman does not wish to have a or another child;" 36 percent agreed in cases of "extreme poverty."

The fact that cases have been brought to court (usually by statutory bodies) coincides with the strategy of the International Planned Parenthood Federation, which has been actively involved in the campaign to introduce new legislation in Northern Ireland.

Cases in which Northern Irish courts have approved abortion—for example, where the mother threatened suicide or had a learning disability—do not prove that the law is unclear. The judges may have delivered perverse judgments, which may create confusion for some and be used to bring the law into disrepute, but this does not mean that the statutes are defective.

What of the women from Northern Ireland who go to England for abortions? Clearly people have the means to travel abroad to do things that are not legal in their own jurisdiction. This will always be the case where different jurisdictions have differing laws. A law intended to permit the killing of the most vulnerable members of the human family is not justified by the fact that others already have such legislation.

In any case, the experience of other countries is that unless abortion is entirely unrestricted it will result in some degree of what pro-abortionists call "exporting the problem." Thus while France has a very permissive policy on early abortion but restrictions on later abortion, two to three thousand French women a year travel for abortions to England, where later gestation abortion is more readily available.

If the purpose of legalizing abortion is to stop women from traveling for abortions, a jurisdiction will have to have the most permissive law anywhere; otherwise some women will still be "forced" to go abroad to have abortions and accusations of "hypocrisy" will persist. Pro-abortionists should give the people of Northern Ireland more credit than to think they would capitulate on their principles to such a miserable tactic.

"The fact that legal abortion provides a beneficial alternative to those who would otherwise have illegal abortions was belied by nine studies. These studies showed that 80-90 percent of the women who have legally induced abortions would not opt for the abortion if it were illegal."—Richard R. Parlour, M.D. & James H. Ford, M.D., Medical Counterpoint

---

It is important to bear in mind that many women who undergo abortions do so unwillingly—under pressure from partners, employers, parents, doctors, and so forth. Legalizing abortion gives a "license" to third parties to pressure expectant mothers toward abortion.

Those who make great play of the trauma suffered by women who travel for abortions totally ignore the trauma that will be suffered by far more women in the jurisdiction if abortion is legalized there. The law in Northern Ireland protects pregnant girls from being marched to the family doctor by parents demanding that an abortion be arranged. This scenario is far from unknown in Britain.

Australia and New Zealand

Barrister Greg Smith, the Australian Crown Prosecutor, comments that the abortion law in Northern Ireland "gives better protection to the unborn and their mothers than any other abortion law operating in common law jurisdictions."

For example, a legislative change in New Zealand in 1977-78, although intended to give greater protection to the unborn, resulted within two years of its enactment in more abortions being performed, and the numbers have continued to increase.

Doctors in New Zealand have found themselves unable to prevent abortions or (in at least one documented case) to ensure the care of a newborn child who survived an abortion.

Using these two nations as examples, any change in Northern Ireland's abortion legislation would only worsen the law, not "improve" it, with regard to protecting unborn children.

Righteousness does not consist in being just a little less bad than our neighbors.

Zimbabwe

The Pro-life Association of Zimbabwe has been in existence for more than ten years. For most of those years, the association operated on a voluntary basis. However, with the increased threats to life the group hired a full-time staff to establish a media center, naming Bob Phiri as director. Below, he describes the state of the pro-life movement in Zimbabwe.

"Last year we successfully defeated an attempt to introduce a liberal abortion law, which had been disguised as a law to assist HIV-positive pregnant women. The U.N. Family Planning Association coerced our government to define a national population policy. The policy document is loosely written in such a way that it could possibly include abortion as a means of population control.

"A process led by civil organizations to write a new constitution for Zimbabwe is gathering momentum. Unfortunately, local radical feminist groups have jumped on the bandwagon with a view of attempting to entrench 'a right to abortion' into the Constitution.

"The World Bank launched its 'safe motherhood' initiative in Zimbabwe last year. This initiative seeks to obtain the institution of liberal abortion laws in Third World countries.

"Euthanasians are carrying on media campaigns locally to convince the nation of the merit of 'merciful deaths.' It was in view of all these increased threats to life that we decided to staff our administration unit on a full-time basis. Our resources are very limited, and we rely on subscriptions and local donations. We also offer material assistance and counseling to women in crisis pregnancy situations."

—Dr. Bob Phiri

When I read e-mails from the Third World, I am very humbled, aren't you? They have so many pressing needs just to survive and yet, if their babies don't survive, they have no future at all.

While in Bosnia in 1994, I asked a doctor in one of the hospitals where we left Samaritan's Purse relief packages about their nation's abortion policy. She said that they had a very liberal abortion policy until the war erupted, and their government rescinded the law. I asked her why. She answered, "We need all our children to remain a nation."

I could not help but think, *Will it take a devastating war on American soil to rescind our killing law?*

Next comes an e-mail from Priests for Life at the Vatican, demonstrating how this clergy organization is fighting for the lives of all the world's children.

The Vatican

> "I am delighted to share my encouragement with you about fighting these three extremely important evils—lack of human rights, abortion, and euthanasia—which attack life at its most vulnerable and defenseless stages. These are also key themes for the work of Priests for Life, an international association that I have been privileged to direct since 1993.
>
> "Dr. Bernard Nathanson, after explaining the strategy he and his colleagues used years ago to launch the abortion rights movement,

declared to an assembly of Catholic priests, 'We would never have gotten away with what we did if you had been united, purposeful, and strong.' He knew then what the promoters of abortion and euthanasia still know, that when the church is fully engaged against the culture of death, the latter cannot prevail.

"That is the purpose and mission of Priests for Life: to provide practical encouragement and the necessary tools to fully activate the structures of the church to proclaim, celebrate, and serve the gospel of life. Through seminars for clergy and extensive networking between clergy and pro-life groups, Priests for Life provides a unique function within the pro-life movement and stands ready to serve each and every group and individual, whether clergy or lay, of any denomination.

"The efforts we are engaged in are not in vain. As the pope once said in a private session, the spoken truth has a power that error can never have, no matter how loudly or widely that error is proclaimed.

"May all who gather together for life issues be sent forth with renewed vigor to your respective countries, carrying out the greatest cause in human history, and doing so with a strength that is not your own. I therefore urge you to do this with the greatest possible confidence and joy."

—Father Frank Pavone

In the 1880s, Charles H. Spurgeon wrote in his devotional *Morning by Evening* the following thoughts based on Colossians 2:6: "If we have received Christ Himself in our inmost hearts, our new life will manifest its intimate acquaintance with Him by *a walk of faith in Him.* Walking implies *action.* Our religion is not to be confined to our closet; we must carry out into practical effect that which we believe.

"If a man walks in Christ, then he so acts as Christ would act; for Christ being in him, his hope, his love, his joy, his life, he is the reflex of the image of Jesus; and men say of that man, 'He is like his Master; he lives like Jesus Christ.'"

We're going to get a look of these who "walk in Christ" in ways we have perhaps never thought of. Getting closer to home brings our faith into perspective.

CHAPTER 17

Closer to Home

Activism is simply taking what is in one's mind and heart and physically acting on it. Activism denotes a living faith, not a subjective, passive faith that is self-centered. Activism has everything to do with accessing the Holy Spirit's direction in the catching of fish and the frying of those fish in the right pan at the right time for the right eaters. The more fish you have to fry, the more hungry ones you have to satisfy.

The disciples had twelve baskets left over when Jesus multiplied their efforts of obedience—enough for the next crowd that might show up. That is why this next "fish parable" is interesting to pro-life activists, because someone has to get the boat, get the line wet, stay through the night if need be, and haul in the load. You can't just talk a fish into the boat.

They Called Themselves Fishermen

A group existed that called themselves fishermen. There were many fish in the waters around. In truth, the whole area was surrounded by streams and lakes filled with fish. And the fish were hungry.

It came to pass that week after week, month after month, and year after year, those who called themselves fishermen met in meetings; they talked about their call to fish, the abundance of fish, and how they might go about fishing.

They carefully analyzed what fishing meant, urged fishing as an occupation, and declared that fishing is always to be a primary task of fishermen. These same fishermen built large, beautiful buildings for local fishing headquarters. Their plea was that everyone should be a fisherman and that every fisherman should fish.

In addition to meeting regularly, they organized a board to send out fishermen to other places where there were many fish. The board was formed by those who had the great vision and courage to speak about fishing, to define fishing, and to promote the idea of fishing in faraway streams and lakes where many fish of different colors swam.

Furthermore, the board hired staff and appointed committees and held many meetings to issue statements on fishing, to agree on what new streams should be thought about. Large, elaborate and expensive training centers were built with the original and primary purpose of teaching fishermen how to fish.

Over the years, courses were offered on the needs of fish, the nature of fish, how to recognize different fish, the psychological reactions of fish, the various backgrounds of fish, and how to approach and feed fish. Those who taught had doctorates in "Fishology."

Further, the fishermen built large printing houses to publish fishing guides. Presses were kept busy day and night to produce materials solely devoted to fishing methods and equipment. Meetings were arranged to talk about fishing. An expert speaker's bureau was also provided to schedule special speakers on the subject of fishing.

Notwithstanding all this activity, it was noted that fishermen themselves did not fish: They pleaded for fishing. The boards did not fish: They planned for fishing. The teachers of Fishology did not fish: They explained fishing. The expert speakers did not fish: They preached about fishing.

However, after one stirring address on "The Necessity of Fishing," one young man left the meeting and went fishing. The next day he reported that he had caught two outstanding fish. He was honored for his excellent catch and scheduled to visit all the big meetings possible to tell how he had done it.

In fact, he quit his fishing in order to have time to tell about the experience to the other fishermen. He was also placed on the Fishermen's General Board as a person having considerable experience.

Now, many of the fishermen made sacrifices and put up with all kinds of difficulties. Few were well paid for their service on the boards and training centers. Some lived near the water and bore the smell of dead fish. They received the ridicule of some that made fun of their fishermen's clubs and the fact that they claimed to be fishermen, yet never fished. They had doubts about those who felt it was of little use to attend and talk about fishing.

After all, were they not following the one who said: "Follow me, and I will make you fishers of men" (Matthew 4:19)?

It came about that one day someone made the outlandish suggestion that those who did not fish were not actually fishermen—no matter how much they claimed to be. Someone actually asked: "Is a person a fisherman if year after year he never catches (or even tries to catch) a fish? If he is not fishing, can he be following?"

Those who called themselves fishermen, and their boards and committees and training centers and speakers, were all very hurt by that question.

Are you a *real* fisherman?

Nehemiah at the Wall

Here's an inspiring reminder from another activist:

> "Have you, like me, noticed that recent media reports seem to be aimed at frightening the Church of Jesus Christ into inaction? If we just keep out of the streets, out of social issues like abortion, out of world affairs, and stick to our potluck suppers, we can avoid persecution. If we persist in being an active and living Church, a change agent in our society, we will pay the price of meddling. This sounds so familiar.

"When Nehemiah was rebuilding the wall, Sanballat and company tried to get him to quit too. They sent threatening reports and accused him of what he had not done. His response was the following:

"'Then I sent a message to him saying, "Such things as you are saying, have not been done, but you are inventing them in your own mind." For all of them were trying to frighten us, thinking, "They will become discouraged with the work and it will not be done." But now, O God, strengthen my hands.'

"Nehemiah did not believe the bad reports meant to frighten him, because he had a job to do and would not allow himself to be distracted. We also have a job to do. We cannot be distracted by bad reports meant to frighten us into inaction. We must stand and build the wall.

"What is the wall God has appointed you to build? What are the 'bad reports' sent to frighten you and make you retreat? Remember who sent you and who is the accuser of the brethren, then ask God to strengthen your hands."

—Pat McEwen

The Gates of Hell

The next three e-mails concern a young Bible school student, John Reyes. They tell the story of what it means to stand for Christ, for the unborn, for those without a voice, even if it is only arranging for other activists to do kingdom work!

After getting the e-mail from Flip Benham, I wrote to John Reyes to get an update and met a most gracious young man. Sometimes we must visit our own in jail, send gifts, and raise prayers, consciences, and petition unjust courts.

Here is a summary of the events that landed John and Flip in jail:

> On November 9, 1997, a rally was held at Liberty University concerning the "God Is Going Back to School Campaign." The call that night was to take the gospel of Jesus Christ to E. C. Glass High School by way of the public sidewalk.
>
> There were about thirty Liberty students who came to the altar to commit to be a witness in the morning. Flip Benham, director of Operation Rescue National, and John Reyes, national director of Students Active for Life & Truth (SALT), a pro-life group at Liberty University, and coordinator for Operation Rescue National, were both surprised and encouraged when around three hundred Liberty students showed up to proclaim that Jesus Christ is Lord at E. C. Glass High School.
>
> This group stood on the public sidewalk and sang praise songs to our Lord, passed out literature, and witnessed to the students as they

entered the school. There were five high school students who came to know Jesus Christ that day. There were no arrests.

At one point, Flip was asked to move off of school property. He immediately complied with them and began moving the large group across the street where they prayed and dispersed for the morning.

Once again, there were no arrests. It is interesting to note that the principal at E. C. Glass High School would not allow her students to pray during the "See You at the Pole" campaign because they did not have a permit.

Several weeks later, a grand jury was convened, and Flip and John were indicted for trespass, disorderly conduct, and parading without a permit. William G. Petty, the Commonwealth Attorney, and Judge Richard Miller, being unable to refute the truth of the gospel message, chose to attack the messengers.

On February 17, 1998, Flip and John were found guilty of trespass even though the police department testified that the demonstrators complied with everything the police asked. They were found "not guilty" on the other two charges. Judge Miller handed down the maximum allowable sentence of one year in jail and a five-hundred dollar fine. He did suspend six months of that sentence.

When told the appeal process would start the following day, the judge responded, "It will not do him any good, because I am not allowing him to leave the state." Rather than sit in Lynchburg while the appeal is pending, Flip Benham began his jail time the next day. He did not want to be apart from his family any longer than necessary.

In the meantime, John has been told by the Commonwealth that he would not be able to leave Virginia until the case is closed. It has been almost two years since the trial. The Commonwealth's attorney told John that if he agreed to an increased bond, from three thousand to seventy-five hundred dollars, then they would permit him to visit his family in Connecticut. Because he is a full-time student (majoring in biblical studies), John does not have the money to afford to pay the difference. John is now a prisoner of the State of Virginia, bound by its borders.

John is going to try to finish school before he serves his time. He is preparing to be a minister of the gospel and has never been in trouble a day in his life. One year in jail is outrageous for a first offense. Judicial tyrants have once again attacked the Body of Christ. We must respond while we still have the freedom to do so.

This was sent out by Flip Benham after the appeals process ended:

On August 12, we received word that our wonderful friend in Christ, John Reyes, had lost his challenge to an absolutely outrageous sentence in the Supreme Court of the State of Virginia. John was the student coordinator who, in November 1997, helped us organize more than three hundred students from Liberty University to bring the gospel of Jesus Christ to the E. C. Glass High School in Lynchburg, Virginia. For this heinous act and John's courageous stand for King Jesus, he was awarded a six-month jail sentence.

John has not been allowed to leave Virginia for the past two years awaiting the outcome of his appeal. You will remember that there were no arrests made by the Lynchburg police when the students were at E. C. Glass.

The police officers all commented on the orderly, well-behaved manner in which the Liberty students conducted themselves. It was only after school superintendent James McCormick convinced a grand jury that these students should be tried on misdemeanor trespass charges that we were brought to trial in Lynchburg. It was a fiasco!

It became very clear during the trial that the real problem was not our behavior at the high school but the content of our message that brought the true offense to Mr. McCormick. We had dared to say that his high school had become the very "gates of hell."

> This could not be tolerated and, therefore, I was privileged to serve several months in the Lynchburg City Jail. Now it is John's turn.
>
> He has told me he is ready to do whatever is necessary to bring glory and honor to His Lord who despised the shame and hung naked on a Cross. This is exactly what I would expect from John Reyes. He is a young man of courage and conviction who was hoping to finish his degree at Liberty this fall semester. If it is inevitable that John must go to jail in Lynchburg, it is imperative that he not go alone.
>
> Keep pressing the gates of hell, in Jesus' name!
>
> *—Flip Benham*

What I am most concerned about at times is the lack of spiritual leadership on the spiritual battlefield. How do we replace those who are out for a time? Who trains them, loves them, gives them the example to emulate as they find their own place in the kingdom?

For these concerns, I asked Roger Domingo to send some guidelines on how to educate the clergy, our church leaders. They have the anointing and authority to move the mountains on all fronts that beset the church. What follows are his suggestions.

Enlightening the Clergy

The education of the clergy must begin with the same crash course required for society, the Church, and the pro-life movement: Abortion is the defining battle of a current worldwide culture war. Babies are human; abortion is murder.

It is not a problem of degree, as in a government's less-than-enthusiastic "war on drugs" or "war on poverty," both godly goals imperfectly pursued. It is rather a repudiation of the godly standard and an aggressive establishment of an abomination that is needed.

Chemical abortion is rapidly eclipsing surgical abortion, and even pro-life leadership is failing to adjust to this change. Previous "pro-life champions" are shrinking back from declaring the abortifacient essence of The Pill and other drugs so willingly ordered by the doctor.

There are other specific messages just for the clergy, like: "A holocaust is raging on your watch!"

History (and God) will judge today's leaders as harshly as it condemns the sins of silence during the abolition of slavery, Nazism, and apartheid that ruled so long in open view.

"Prophets and priests alike, all practice deceit. They dress the wound of my people as though it were not serious. 'Peace, peace,' they say, when there is no peace." (Jeremiah 6:13-14)

The key is to enlighten and enlist the leadership of the clergy first, then the laity.

Pastors and prophets are dissimilar beings in their gifting. It is historically ignorant to expect pastors en masse—or even individually without the assurance of strong support—to risk the congregational schism and fiscal disaster that bold pro-life action might spawn.

Pastors almost never "lead" until a mass movement of the flock is clearly under way. This is where we come in to support and assist in all ways possible. When a leader asks you to help organize or make calls to cover the situation—or whatever—be there to do it.

Three steps laymen can and must take in order to conscript the clergy into the life issues movement are the following:

1. Take a bold political stand by issuing a personal pro-life "declaration of dependence upon God" to their pastor and all members of government who represent them or who exercise control over their lives.

2. Wear a pro-life emblem that keeps their strong pro-life stand a constant factor in their day-to-day social interaction.

3. Politely demand that the pastor and the local church take an unequivocal and incessant pro-life position, defending the sacredness of life and advancing pro-life causes. If a pastor steadfastly refuses to take such a

stand, the conscientious Christian must pray about investing his or her time and resources there or within a decidedly life-fostering fellowship.

Section VI

Heroes of the Faith

Chapter 18

Testimonies

At last we come to the testimonies of some of the heroes in the life issues movement. You have been reading all along what many others have done and said, all heroes in God's eyes.

We are beginning with one who has taken a dark time in his own life and turned it into glorious light for all. Charles Colson has a deep love and affection for the Lord Jesus Christ. I remember meeting him one time in Orlando when he was appearing on behalf of his new book. Activist Sharon Turner stopped in her tracks in the busy aisle, came to ramrod attention, and saluted Chuck Colson. He was obviously touched and received the honor of that moment. He stopped, drew away from the small crowd around him, and saluted her back in total seriousness.

When you have been in the battle, you come to recognize the generals.

Colson addresses this question: Is there a connection between taking the lives of innocent babies and the escalating crime rate of the world? Would the total devaluation of anyone's life become proof that crime will more than likely go unpunished when certain designated groups are left vulnerable to what was formerly a crime?

Chuck Colson of Prison Ministries Fellowship has made this connection in the following essay. In addition, he gives many recommendations for activism in the fight for life.

Smiling Fascism

by Charles Colson

Does abortion reduce the crime rate?

That's the question Americans have been asking as we've read news reports of a new study linking the drop in youth crime to the legalization of abortion a generation ago.

Pro-life groups immediately attacked the study as badly flawed. But the real question is not whether the study is true. The question is, Do we attack the roots of crime—or do we attack unborn babies?

The study is called "Legalized Abortion and Crime," and University of Chicago economist Steven Levitt and Stanford law professor John Donohue authored it. The study indicates, for example, that in the five states that legalized abortion ahead of the Supreme Court's 1973 *Roe v. Wade* ruling, crime started falling slightly earlier than in other parts of the country. And the study found that states that had especially high rates of abortion in the first years after Roe tended to experience especially large recent declines in crime, even when other factors were considered.

The authors attribute this drop in crime to the fact that in the years after abortion was legalized, the majority of women seeking abortions were poor, young, unmarried, and minority. Well, Christians shouldn't be surprised that a drop in the number of children born to single and underclass women might reduce crime.

We know that high proportions of the young men who commit the most serious crimes are born to the kind of mothers Donohue and Levitt said were having abortions in the 1970s.

The question is, What do we do with this information?

Well, first, we ought to be aware of how studies like these can lead to unspeakable evil. For example, in the 1920s Planned Parenthood founder Margaret Sanger called for the elimination through sterilization of what she called "inferior races" and "morons, misfits, and the maladjusted." Sanger blamed them for most of the crime in society.

Hitler's death camps for "inferior races" revealed where eugenics leads. Yet today eugenics is returning in new forms. For example, when testing reveals a Down syndrome baby, doctors often pressure parents to abort. Not surprisingly, eight out of ten do. In one study, a third of the mothers said they felt "more or less forced" to abort. And now, subtly and quietly, this study tries to plant in the public mind the idea that abortion is a social good—that it stops future crime. It's the Third Reich all over again.

Well, we ought to be reminding folks of the great forgotten story of Planned Parenthood: that it was started for the horrendous purpose of getting rid of the "unfit" and producing a better class of people. The abortion lobby does not want to admit this—and that's why it's been so quiet about this study. But you and I should press the point home.

As Christians, we need to demonstrate that there's a much better way to combat social ills than imitating Adolph Hitler. Instead of building abortion clinics in poor neighborhoods as Planned Parenthood does, we ought to intervene in the lives of desperate women and their children.

We should support programs like Angel Tree, which brings the love of Christ to the crime-prone children of prisoners. We ought to support Crisis Pregnancy Centers and imitate people like the Rev. Eugene Rivers in Boston and criminologist John Dilulio in Philadelphia, who are leading efforts to help at-risk kids finish high school and find jobs.

In the process, we'll demonstrate that the answer to crime is not killing more babies, but bringing the love of Christ to those in need.

* * * * *

One of the people who helped formulate the prayer for the girl-child is Kurt Dillinger, who along with his wife, Gayle, have been on the forefront of establishing crisis pregnancy centers first in Michigan, then expanding globally to instruct and help others to do the same.

At one time a pastor, Dillinger allowed God to touch his heart deeply over the waste of priceless lives being incinerated, bludgeoned, scissored, crushed, chemically burned, and dismembered while still living. This is the real side of abortion: Mothers who need real help and a place to turn. These thoughts are taken from Kurt's speech at an international conference.

A War on Compassion

by Kurt Dillinger

It is an honor to be invited to this conference and be in the presence of such distinguished guests. As I was introduced to some of you, I found myself asking the question, Why am I here?

My first response to that question was, I'm here primarily because I'm in love. I'm in love with Jesus my Lord and Savior, and I have decided to follow Him wherever He leads me. In practice, that may look like following Bert Dorenbos!

My second response to that question was, I'm committed to doing my best in communicating the Lord's heart concerning life issues, the very issues that demand so much of our time, energy and resources. These issues the Lord has already solved. We are simply called to listen well and follow with reckless abandon. He is faithful in showing the way.

Do you believe this? The Lord is actively networking the nations for His purposes for life, because He has said, "I am the way, the truth and the life." We are all called to do our designated parts, and our part is revealed to us on our knees.

On the subject assigned to me today, here are some thoughts. The character of a nation is defined by how it provides and protects its most vulnerable innocent. Its character secures the future of the nation. To some nations, character is of no value, and its innocent are dispensable. The future of such a nation is certain economic, moral, and spiritual deprivation and rapid decline. That nation will eventually destroy itself from the inside out, which is a direct reflection of abortion.

The abortion practice in America is built upon deception. This is clearly illustrated by the historic case *Roe v. Wade.* In a [radio] interview, Norma McCorvey (Roe) announced, "I'm pro-life. I think I've always been pro-life. I just didn't know it."

McCorvey claimed that she had been raped and was pregnant when she approached attorney Sarah Weddington about suing for the right to have an abortion. McCorvey never had an abortion, because the decision came too late. She carried the baby to term and gave it up for adoption. McCorvey later admitted that she had not been raped.

ABC's *World News Tonight* and *Nightline* featured exclusive interviews with McCorvey in which she renounced her role in the abortion advocacy movement and declared that abortion is wrong. "I think abortion is wrong. I think what I did with *Roe v. Wade* was wrong, and I just have to take a pro-life position on [abortion]."

I quote from Norma McCorvey:

"Abortion has been founded on lies and deception from the very beginning. All I did was lie about how I got pregnant. I was having an affair. It all started out as a little lie. I said what I needed to say. But my 'little lie' grew and grew and became more horrible with each telling. Sarah and Linda's (the pro-abortion attorneys in Roe) eyes seemed blinded to my obvious inability to tell the same story twice. It was good for the cause. It read well in the newspapers. With the help of willing media and the credibility of well-known columnists, the lie became known as 'the truth' these past 25 years."

One of the most common arguments abortion advocates make in defense of legal abortion is that making abortion illegal will cause women to go to the "back alleys" and obtain unsafe abortions. They cite how thousands of women died as a result of unsafe abortions before abortion was legalized through the *Roe v. Wade* U.S. Supreme Court decision.

Dr. Bernard Nathanson, long ago cofounder of the National Abortion Rights Action League (NARAL), admits his group lied about the number of women who died of illegal abortions when testifying before the Supreme Court in 1972. Dr. Nathanson admitted that he and others in the abortion rights movement intentionally fabricated the number of women who allegedly died as a result of illegal abortions.

"How many deaths were we talking about when abortion was illegal? In NARAL, we generally emphasized the drama of the individual case, not the mass statistics, but when we spoke of the latter it was always five thousand to ten thousand deaths a year. I confess that I knew the figures were totally false, and I suppose the others did too if they stopped to think of it. But in the 'morality of the revolution,' it was a useful figure, widely accepted, so why go out of our way to correct it with honest statistics? The overriding concern was to get the laws eliminated, and anything within reason that had to be done was permissible."

Today in Trinidad West Indies, abortion laws are being drafted based on the "back alley" argument. They base their argument on the practice of distributing an overdose of medication used for the treatment of ulcers. This is a single example of how abortion is spreading around the globe.

* * * * *

More recently, Ron Fitzsimmons, executive director of the National Coalition of Abortion Providers in Alexandria, Virginia, admitted he "lied through my teeth" when he said that partial-birth abortions were performed rarely, only when the mother's life was in danger or the fetus was malformed. He also admitted that pro-lifers are correct in their assertion that the procedure is common.

In most cases, he said, partial-birth abortion is performed on women who are five months pregnant with a healthy fetus—and that both the pro-abortion and pro-life factions are aware of this. Like Nathanson and his colleagues, he lied for the cause, until he became convinced that the debate on the issue should be based on the truth.

The deception continues.

Clearly, a war is raging in America and around the globe. It's a war on compassion. A war fixed on destroying the image of God.

I want to spend my time on what I believe to be the truth.

* * * * *

For our next essay on implementing activism, we go to a powerful leader in pro-life, Joe Scheidler of Pro-Life Action League in Chicago, Illinois.

This method of activism is one he learned on the frontlines in Brooklyn and Queens, New York, from Monsignor Philip J. Reilly and Sister Dorothy Rothar, who teach sidewalk counseling all over the world. She is a former teacher, and very strict! When she tells you to stand across the street and pray, that's what you do.

She'll run here and there, softly calling to the women, loving them in such immediate crises. "Sidewalk counseling is really evangelism," Sister Dorothy told us.

While Catholics often use rosaries to give to the mothers, Protestants and evangelicals may wish to substitute a small cross as the symbolic connection. The main point, however, is that prayer support allows the power of the Lord to enter into a difficult situation.

Surely every Christian who wants to become an activist for life can become disciplined in prayer as a launching point.

What is most powerful is connecting with the Father of all, the Creator of the Universe, the Lover of humanity's souls, to know Him who rescues us from the death sin brings by the blood sacrifice of His Son, Jesus Christ. We have but to believe it, and act on it.

Here's how Joe tells it.

Sidewalk Counseling Is Really Evangelism

by Joe Scheidler

You'll find it hard to believe what the priest in the green windbreaker and the nun with the straw hat accomplished. I would have trouble believing it myself if I hadn't seen it with my own eyes. I feel as if I've witnessed the multiplication of the loaves and fishes. I've seen a miracle. I've always believed in the power of prayer, but I believe in it now in a whole new way.

Did something ever happen to you that was so profound, so powerful, so amazing, that it transformed the way you looked at everything? That's what happened to me earlier this month in New York.

You see, I took five of our top sidewalk counselors to New York to see the priest in the green windbreaker and the nun in the straw hat in action at a notorious Brooklyn abortion mill. I had heard that the priest, Monsignor Philip J. Reilly, and the nun, Sister Dorothy Rothar, closed twenty-two abortion mills in the

Brooklyn/Queens area, converted dozens of abortion mill workers, and talked some of the most hard-core abortion-bound women out of killing their babies. It sounded too good to be true.

I prayed while Monsignor Reilly and Sister Dorothy talked to the pregnant mothers and accomplices entering the extermination center. Using the prayer book assembled by Monsignor Reilly, our group became absorbed in prayer. Our hearts were so warmed by the mysteries of the rosary and the litany and by singing some of the beautiful old hymns that we didn't want to be interrupted for anything. It was as if we were already in heaven.

Dozens of pregnant mothers approached the abortion mill and went inside. Three were so hard-boiled, they seemed beyond hope. I didn't think there was a chance Monsignor Reilly would convert these three, but I prayed: "Lord, if Father Reilly can convert these three, I'll know You're touching the hardest of hearts with Your love in response to our prayers at this moment."

One of the three, a young Jewish woman dressed in black, had cursed Monsignor Reilly as she entered death's door. She came out after a few minutes and hugged Sister Dorothy. (Father Reilly was busy talking to another woman when she came out.)

Another woman was dressed in leather and wore an orange top. "This gal—no way," I thought. Ten minutes later, she came out of the abortion mill in tears and hugged Monsignor Reilly. The third girl was black, dressed in a striped outfit. She was with a black man and yelled at Father Reilly while entering the mill.

About fifteen minutes later they came out, seeking pro-life help.

I will share with you something personal. I have seen the hand of God. I have witnessed the unfolding of a miracle. I have watched in amazement while praying for things to happen *as they were happening!* That day, thirty-seven pregnant mothers changed their hearts and chose life, one of them a Catholic who said she wanted to return to the sacrament of confession. That day we deprived the abortion industry of more than fifteen thousand dollars in fees. It's almost beyond belief.

Even though some babies died at the abortion mill that day, remember that no one wants to die alone. We stood watch with these condemned, abandoned children at the hour of their death, prayed for them, and loved them—the only kindness they ever knew on Earth.

Let me give you the essence of their method. There's no confrontation, no shouting, and no anger—only a low-key, charitable offer to help, supported by prayers and hymns. But they use a powerful tool: blessed rosaries. When a woman approaches a mill, he puts a rosary in her hand and says, "Look, if you need any help, we're here to help you. God loves you. He cares about you and your baby."

He puts a rosary into the hand of the accomplice (the pregnant woman's companions), and tells him or her to pray a rosary that she'll do the right thing. If the woman is already inside, he tells the accomplice to go inside because "she'll need you. Give her this literature. She needs it." Bear in mind that Father Reilly is supported by several teams of prayer warriors while all this is going on—one prayer team right there at the mill itself. Other teams pray in convents, chapels, or in homes.

Prayer support is the key to the method.

Father Reilly says the abortion-bound pregnant mothers are not our enemies nor are the abortion-mill workers, because as sinners, we're all in the same boat. Let's face it: We've all been in morally dangerous situations where we could have benefited if someone had handed us some information. Satan is our enemy, because he is committed to evil and cannot repent.

Here in Chicago, we've saved thousands of babies from abortion using our method of sidewalk counseling, but now I want to incorporate the method developed by Monsignor Reilly and his helpers to save even more women and their babies.

The truth is, the abortion catastrophe will be solved by massive conversions—massive, ongoing daily repentance. Never before has there been a more urgent need to bring people back to God. As Monsignor Reilly told us, "If you convert the mother, you also save the baby."

Here's my plan inspired by what the Lord showed me in New York. I use *99 Ways to Stop Abortion* (the title of my book), but sidewalk counseling has always been the Pro-Life Action League's number one program. Here in Chicago, we've already begun implementing Monsignor Reilly's method, and we saved three babies at the Albany abortion mill the first time we tried it. We'll save more as we develop more prayer support.

In the fall, I flew Monsignor Reilly into Chicago to present a workshop on how to apply his method, and he led a field training exercise at a Chicago mill. From coast to coast I will continue to preach and teach sidewalk counseling at all my speaking engagements, but now I'll also promote Monsignor Reilly's program.

I believe in my heart that this method of sidewalk counseling can bring the abortion industry to its knees. Make no mistake: We care about the pregnant mother and we're determined to bring her back to God. Fifteen centuries ago, St. Benedict summarized what needs to be done: *Ora et labora.* Pray and work. The Pro-Life Action League has the infrastructure and contacts to promote and spread this astonishing method throughout the land.

"I counsel you to buy from me gold refined in the fire, so you can become rich; and white clothes to wear, so you can cover your shameful nakedness; and salve to put on your eyes, so you can see. Those whom I love I rebuke and discipline. So be earnest, and repent. Here I am! I stand at the door and knock. If anyone hears my voice and opens the door, I will come in and eat with him, and he with me. To him who overcomes, I will give the right to sit with me on my throne, just as I overcame and sat down with my Father on his throne. He who has an ear, let him hear what the Spirit says to the churches." (Revelation 3:18-22)

The Hand of God

A Comment From Bernard Nathanson

Probably the most effective activism that Christians can involve themselves in is evangelization—the introduction of the kingdom of Jesus Christ through His shed blood for their sins. Once unbelievers become disciplined Christians, their hearts change from the inside. The Holy Spirit deals with self-centered hostilities. When there is obedience, holiness results and with that, a marked decrease in the lust to enter deathtraps.

One such example is the conversion of Dr. Bernard Nathanson, who personally performed more than seventy-five thousand abortions. For two years he was director of the world's largest abortion clinic in New York City. The facility was open from 8 a.m. to midnight, seven days a week, and performed more than a hundred abortions a day.

Yet this same doctor who once strongly argued for safe and legal abortion could not live with the results of what he practiced and preached. Dr. Nathanson eventually changed his position (as a result of seeing an embryo in the womb through a new invention at the time, ultrasound), and lived twenty years after that with regret as an abortionist.

In his book *The Hand of God,* Dr. Nathanson outlines how, after being pro-life for many years, he actually found Jesus Christ.

This interview is taken from *Physicians' Magazine,* published by *Focus on the Family.* Another of our greatest heroes is Dr. James Dobson. What a warrior for life issues he has proven to be!

Dr. Nathanson speaks:

"The short answer (to how this happened) is that my life had spun out of control. I knew I was not capable of controlling or directing my life anymore. I had made a mess of it. I'd been married and divorced three times, my family life was a wreck, and I had hurt so many people on my march to what I thought was success. I just couldn't handle my life anymore. I had to turn it over to somebody who could. And the only person I knew that could take care of me was Jesus."

Dr. Nathanson's book also explains the remarkable story of how he produced *The Silent Scream,* which has turned thousands around to a pro-God, pro-life view, all because he was truly changed from the inside.

Let the word of Christ richly dwell within you, with all wisdom teaching and admonishing one another with psalms and hymns and spiritual songs, singing with thankfulness in your hearts to God. (Colossians 3:16, NAS)

Thankfulness Might Mean Life

by Keith Tucci

Thankfulness is the fuel in the tank of the believer. It is the cement that brings the whole Church together. It is the witness that there is still hope in our land and in our world and in our lives.

Like you, over the years I've had to dig deep and reach high to cheer myself up so I could keep running the race. Christian bookstores and secular bookstores are filled with volumes on how to be happy, yet most of them are attempts at window dressing rather than dealing with the heart issue.

Thankfulness, on the other hand, goes to the core. It affects our spiritual value system. People that abound in thankfulness, quite simply, are hard to stop.

Just months after I surrendered my life to Jesus Christ on a Pittsburgh street corner, the pastor of the church my new Christian friends had brought me to asked me to pray about coming to church early and picking up some of our senior saints who were having transportation problems.

Pray about it? Was he kidding? I was so thankful that I would have gone out and laid in the middle of the street if I thought it would help somebody. I didn't need to pray. Of course I would.

That decision, of course, meant that I had to be there early. I couldn't miss church or those dear people would also miss. It also gave me great time of fellowship, while driving in that van, with those dear people who had lived through the depression, World War II, and their own heartbreak and tragedies. It was from them that thankfulness was modeled for me.

The day our pastor asked me to drive that van I went home—and cried. The thought of Jesus allowing me to do anything in His name was a humbling thought. Yes, there are days when I still get too big for my britches and act like I am doing God and others a favor, but that attitude can't stand in the face of a thankful life.

One of the weapons of spiritual warfare is thankfulness. Unfortunately, in many cases, it's grown rusty from lack of use, where it would be foolhardy and spiritual suicide to pretend everything is OK. The truth is, we have much to be thankful for, in spite of the heartache the pro-life ministry carries with it.

I am thankful my eyes have been opened. I am thankful for the assurance of my salvation. I am thankful that I have the opportunity to love my unborn neighbor. I am thankful for every life that's been spared. I am thankful for all the opportunities to represent Jesus.

Please understand, this thankfulness, even at this position in my life, is an act of faith first, not a built-in attitude of my own. It's so great to see more and more that thankful people are faithful people who keep pressing on.

I know I've jokingly said—sometimes more truthfully than I'd like to admit—that I wish I had never known about the child-killing tragedy. Yet, when I get alone with the Lord, I am grateful that He would allow me to represent Him for the little ones.

As I sit here sharing my heart, I wonder what would happen if every pro-lifer entered into genuine thankfulness. I am not suggesting some easy cure-all that requires no faith, no work, and no perseverance.

What I am saying is this: If we go forward on a basis of honoring God, for the principle of serving Him, we are going to get a lot farther and have a much better time getting there.

Empty Playgrounds

by Norma L. McCorvey

We received a late fax from Norma McCorvey of Roe No More Ministry and appreciate the deep things the Lord has done in her life. Norma, of course, is the "Jane Roe" in the *Roe v. Wade* Supreme Court case that legalized the killing of pre-born children in America.

In this heartfelt poem, allow Norma to speak to you of the pain she carries and her personal knowledge of "where all the children went."

I sit across from a playground
that I visited this eve with a small child.
I know of such places where children play.
I know that I am the cause of them
not being here today.
These playgrounds for "innocent children"
now dead because of sins I helped do.
I hope, Lord, that the wonderful playgrounds

are well guarded with angels;
angels who will protect them,
keep them happy and safe.
Angels who will make them smile and laugh
So that when that glorious day comes,
the children will not hold "this sin" against me.
For every time I see a playground empty,
I will know that Yours will be full.
The sun is now setting, and my heart hurts, Lord.
For the numbers who from abortion
have been torn apart.
I pray You can put them back together
and make them whole.
If you like, Lord, use my body to make
Your precious children whole again.
I ask You to do this—not only for them, Lord—
But also for the love I have for each of them.
Lord God, You gave Your only Son,
And He died and shed His blood for us all.
All I did was give my baby away,
so that "women could tear theirs apart;"
For this, I will never be able to look into Your
face without shame.

Extremism: A Hallmark of Christianity

by Randall Terry

This is a label nearly as bad as the Scarlet Letter in many American Christian minds; hostile unbelievers cast this insult like the first "without sin" stone on anyone who dares to take an uncompromising stand on issues.

The blackballing of extremists has been so effective that tepid Christian leaders in pastorates, seminaries, and ministry leadership positions have joined Christianity's enemies and launched their own quiet, thoughtful, reasoned attack on extremism.

The result is that battalions of young Davids sit fidgeting on the sidelines, while the Sauls of the church explain to them why it's not God's will to fight Goliath.

However, the charge of extremism, rather than an accusation to be ashamed of, may be an accolade to relish and revel in. In many ways, Christianity is the ultimate paradigm of extremes. No other religion, no other faith, no other deity even comes close. The war on extremism from inside or outside Christianity is ultimately a war on Christianity itself.

Consider the extremes of Christ's attributes and offices:

He is the Lamb of God; He is the Lion of the tribe of Judah. He is the Prince of Peace; He is the Man of War. A bruised reed He will not break; He shatters the nations with a rod of iron. Jesus weeps; He has eyes of fire. He does not lift up His voice; out of His mouth goes a two-edged sword. Christ is the Savior; Christ is the Judge. He made Himself a servant; He is Master and Lord of all. His kingdom is not of this world; He is the King of kings and all kings will bow at His feet. He wore a crown of thorns; He offers a crown of life. He is fully God; He is fully man. These "extremes" nearly tore the church apart.

Consider God the Father:

God is love; God is a consuming fire. God is light; God dwells in the thick darkness. Jacob He loves; Esau He hates.

Consider how extreme Christianity is in our lives and relationships:

The Bible demands that we love our enemies; the psalmist boasts of his perfect hatred for God's enemies. Christ promised to leave His peace with us; He declared that He did not come to bring peace, but a sword. Christ brings unity to Gentile and Jew; He divides a mother-in-law from her daughter-in-law. He commands us to rejoice evermore; He adjures us to let our joy be turned to sorrow, our laughter to weeping.

God's dealings with men and nations are equally extreme:

He will save the city for the sake of ten righteous men; He destroys tens of thousands for the sin of one man. One errant son loses paradise by one act; one obedient Son redeems the world by one act. God forgives the woman taken in adultery; He kills the man for steadying the Ark of the Covenant. He sends blistering drought in Elijah's day; He drowns the world in Noah's. God brought the first son of David and Bathsheba to the grave; He brought their next son to the throne. The angels rejoice when sinners are converted; converted sinners will judge the angels.

Consider biblical heroes; they pulse in extremes:

David is the sweet psalmist of Israel writing poetry; David is the fierce warrior who presents Goliath's head to the king. Elijah stands and conquers four hundred prophets of Baal; he flees in terror at the word of one woman. Abraham begs God for a son; he willingly offers him as a sacrifice until God intervenes. Peter declares he will die for Jesus; within hours he denies he even knows Him. Timid Gideon begs God for a sign; brave Gideon slays two kings on a stone. Saul seeks to kill Christians; he is finally killed for being one.

The extremes of Christianity may startle us, they may make us uncomfortable, but they are not contradictions. The tightrope walker that balances his act with a long pole holds but one pole. It is the use of the extremes of that pole which keeps him in balance. Should he favor one side of the pole and lop off the other, he could not maintain his balance—he would fall.

This is the plight of modern divines and Christian leaders. Having accepted the false notion of Christianity's enemies that certain aspects of our God and faith are extreme (and therefore extremely embarrassing), they have lopped off the extremities that preserve them on precarious heights—and they have fallen; fallen into the safety net of fallen man's opinions, and they have found it a snare. Having turned from the harsh master who reaps what he did not sow, they have enslaved themselves to harsher masters who sow the wind and reap the whirlwind.

Our modern, sophisticated, would-be "heroes of the faith" slay no tyrants, conquer no kingdoms, and risk no martyrdom. Instead, they are photographed with tyrants, protect the status quo of kingdoms, and martyr the reputations of their extremist brethren.

By trying to blend the heat of God's mercy and the coldness of His judgment, the "balanced" have exchanged their glory for the similitude of a politically correct ox; they have bowed before a lukewarm, false deity to be spewed out of Christianity's mouth. By forced blending of God's unapproachable light and the thick darkness in which He dwells, the so-called "moderates" have created the drab-gray God who neither inspires wonder nor invokes dread. They have "balance"—the "balance" of the fixed, lifeless statue.

One achieves healthy balance by remembering both the goodness and severity of God, not by blending them into divine indifference. One maintains balance by embracing the extremes of black and white—not by creating a bland, gray divinity. What Christianity's detractors inside and outside the Church must accept is that Christianity is extreme—extreme to the wildest degree.

Perhaps nothing reveals this extremism more than the final state of man. The righteous live in nightless light; the wicked are cast into outer darkness. The redeemed dwell in perpetual joy; the rebels weep and gnash their teeth forever. Those who have Jesus have eternal life; those who don't have Jesus have eternal damnation. It doesn't get any more extreme than this.

Those who reject extremism must inevitability reject Christ and Christianity.

By rejecting the extremes of male and female, our seminaries have created religious eunuchs, barren heralds, neutered ones that cannot reproduce their kind. By castigating Christianity's extremists, they have castrated its vitality.

Unveil the "balanced moderate" who has done anything great in history. They have won no great battles; they have no tragic defeats. They have no boasts; they have no denial. They offer no heads of giants. Their songs are trite, predictable, and uninspiring.

When "moderates" in the Church call for balance, they really want to lop off the embarrassing extremes of Christ, His Church, and His history. But by doing so they make Christianity an embarrassment.

It is no longer, "These men who have turned the world upside down, have come here also!" but, "These men who want a place at the table have come for a meeting." Past enemies of the gospel feared extremist Christians. "Now when they saw the boldness of Peter and John, and perceived that they were unlearned men, ignorant men, they marveled; and they took knowledge of them that they had been with Jesus." Our modern leaders are learned, but not bold. Our enemies marvel that current Christian leaders won't fight for Christianity; they take note that they have been with Balaam.

These new "champions"—pitiful eunuchs—inspire neither dread nor ecstasy, neither joy nor weeping. They inspire nothing, because only extremes inspire people. Mediocrity, gray and bland, inspires no one. They cannot advance and conquer for Christianity, because they cannot even defend her. They are safe, and they are irrelevant. Or worse yet—they are relevant only as religious hostages to be paraded before our enemies like trophies from a conquered kingdom. By the waters of Babylon they have sung skillfully. Unlike the three Hebrew children, they have bowed...deeply.

Conquered brothers, captured sisters, be loosed of the chains of your safe, gray, lukewarm mediocrity. Cease giving succor to the enemy. Your war on extremism is a war on Christianity itself, and you cannot win. Come battle demons with us. Relish the exhilaration of triumphs; curse the hapless defeats. You can only achieve great victories by risking great disasters.

Stop trying to give God a face-lift. He doesn't need your help. Stop trying to amputate the extremes of Christianity that you find so embarrassing.

And now a word to unbelieving rebels: Behold the goodness and severity of God. If you repent and believe the gospel, you will receive forgiveness and mercy from the God who made you and sent His Son to die for you. But if you continue to rebel, you will be judged. If you spurn His mercy, you shall drink the terrifying cup of His wrath forever. Your accusations of Christianity's extremes will taunt you for all eternity.

And finally, to young believers, take this advice: Flee these barren doctors of divinity. They will deliver you from extremes, but they will rob you of your strength to deliver. They will inoculate you from the pain and anguish of childbirth, because they will sterilize you. Better to be in anguished labor for Jesus than to be a quiet gelding for Jesus.

Rejoice in the boundaries of extremism.

Rejoice in the God of extremes.

Stand, therefore, and arm yourself with the extremes of Christianity.

* * * * *

Now, a word of encouragement from Kay Arthur. When you think the bad guys are getting away with murder, Kay has discovered the answer. She told me during a radio interview that she would be happy to contribute to *Issues of Conscience*, so she sent the following from her latest book, *Our Covenant God: Learning to Trust Him.*

God's Way, in God's Timing

by Kay Arthur

Oh, beloved, isn't it reassuring, isn't it comforting to know that our Covenant partner is bound to defend us and to protect us from our enemies? God took care of Saul—in His way and in His time.

Sometimes God's time is right now…while in other situations we won't see His vindication during our days on earth. But we can know it will come in His time. You may want vengeance now—and your enemies may deserve it now—but God will have it His way, in His time.

I have to remind myself of this fact when I look at the evil rulers rearing their ugly heads down through the pages of history, people like Diocletian and Galerius who insanely destroyed anyone they perceived as being in their way and who cruelly persecuted the people of God.

It's so hard to wait for God's timing when I see the wicked seeming to prosper in their fatness of life while they gorge their corrupt appetites by dining on and devouring others far more righteous than they.

Yet God's Word assures us, it is only just for God to repay with affliction those who afflict you and to give relief to you who are afflicted. And to us, as well, when the Lord Jesus shall be revealed from heaven with His mighty angels in flaming fire dealing out retribution to those who do not know God and to those who do not obey the gospel of our Lord Jesus.

And these will pay the penalty of eternal destruction, away from the presence of the Lord and from the glory of His power, when He comes to be glorified in His saints on that day. He will be marveled at among all who have believed—for our testimony to you was believed.

The psalmist tells how he saw the prosperity of the wicked and almost stumbled because of it, "until I came into the sanctuary of God; then I perceived their end." He saw God had set the wicked in slippery places and would cast them into destruction. They would be utterly destroyed in a moment of time, swept away by sudden terrors as God even despised their form. Chapters six to nineteen in Revelation vividly describe His climactic judgment.

Our loving, righteous God is filled with holy wrath and fully capable of taking care of the wicked. Therefore, we must leave that to Him—and we can, beloved, because of covenant.

The Last Word

I am reminded of a passage in Ecclesiastes 11 that tells us to "sow your seed in the morning, and at evening let not your hands be idle, for you do not know which will succeed, whether this or that, or whether both will do equally well."

We are on Earth such a short time. The Trinity has given each person on Earth certain unchangeable parameters—gender, era, family, nation, health, race—that we neither ask for nor control. The whole package is given at birth.

With our "package" we work within those parameters to glorify God our Creator. It is no good for me to wish I had been born in another country, in another century, as another gender, in a higher class, or whatever else may be dreamed up. That did not happen and never will. It simply was not God's will for me.

The contentment of facing life with a basic understanding of who we are leaves us free to use those very parameters to see what God wants us to do. God gives grace to all His creatures. We do not have to fight for a place when we are handed God's place by birth.

That is why it has become so very important to realize that we are in a great family. The very things that distinguish us reveal the variations that please God immensely. The world wants to stamp out and kill these precious variations and does so under many guises: science, social engineering, euthanasia, sustainable population, racial inequities, gender bias, human rights violations, and so on. The wrongly motivated discriminations are innumerable.

When we who value all human life "sow our seed" according to the Bible, whenever and wherever, we bring the very presence of God closer to those trapped in evil situations.

They see a ray of light.

They smell a breath of freedom.

They realize there is a God who loves and cares for *all* His creation.

Appendix A

Contributors

Acao Familiar do Brasil
Dr. Talmir Rodrigues, M.D.
Rua sergipe n. 344
CEP 19030 – 560
Presidente Prudente, S.P., 19030 Brasil
Phone: +5518 2229341 and Fax: +5518 2227722

Advocates For Life Ministries
Paul deParrie, Founder
6304 N.E. Sandy Blvd.
Portland, Oregon 97213
E-Mail: Paul@lifeadvocate.com
Website:www.lifeadvocate.com

Paul deParrie with his staff produces Life Advocate - The Abortion Abolitionist news magazine and other materials. His latest book is "Dark Cures - Have Doctors Lost Their Ethics?" (Lafayette, LA : Huntington House Publishers, 1998). They welcome news and editorial items to be sent via their e-mail address.

The American Center for Law and Justice (ACLJ)
Keith Fournier, J.D., Executive Director
William D. Watkins, Director of Publications
P. O. Box 65248
Virginia Beach, Virginia 23467-5248 USA
Fax: 615.355.9977

Attorney and life advocate Jay Sekulo is the Founder of ACLJ which provides life advocacy services against religious persecution and pro-life issues. They have a national radio program, newsletter, publications and resource materials. "In Defense of Life - Taking a Stand Against the Culture of Death" (Colorado Springs, CO: NavPress, 1996).

American Family Association
Rev. Donald Wildmon, Founder
M. Buddy Smith, Executive Assistant
P. O. Drawer 2440
Tupelo, Mississippi 38803
Phone: 601 844 5036
E-mail: buddy@afa.net

American Life League, Inc.
P. O. Box 1350
Stafford, Virginia 22555
Phone: 540 659 4171 and Fax: 540 659 2586
E-mail: whylife@all.org
Website: www.all.org/whylife.htm

Provides much literature and grassroots activism for life issues. Contact them for resources and assistance.

American Life League Project: STOPP International
Jim Sedlak, Publisher
E-mail: jsedlak@all.org.
Website: www.all.org

Produces "The Ryan Report" which is named for John A. Ryan, T.O.P., who was one of the first ones to speak out against Margaret Sanger and focuses on the happenings of Planned Parenthood as it affects the family and life issues.

Arzte für das Leben e. V.
Inglof Schmid-Tannwald, President
Perusastrasse 3
80335 München, Germany
Phone/Fax: +49 89 595744
E-Mail:
Ingolf.Schmid-Tannwald@gyn.med.uni-muenchen.de

Australian Federation of Right to Life
GPO Box 3612
2001 Sydney, Australia
Phone: +61 22 998172 and Fax: +61 22 901135
Be'ad Chaim - Israel Pro-life Association (In English)

Ted Walker
Post Office Box 7974
91078 Jerusalem, Israel
Phone/Fax: +97 22 6242516
E-mail: prolife@Netvision.net.il
Website: www.cmrc.on.ca/ProlifeIsrael/welcome.htm

Be'ad Chaim is an Israeli-based crisis pregnancy and pro-life education center instrumental in bringing the gospel to the nation of Israel. Their center is right downtown Jerusalem, saving babies, helping women and bringing awareness to saving lives. They have several materials, videos, and a free newsletter.

Be'ad Chaim Werkgroep Nederland (In Dutch)
t.n.v. T. en W. Kolman
Zwinglilaan 48
1216 Hilversum, Holland
Phone/Fax: +035.624.4150
E-mail: tkolman@worldonline.nl
Internet:
http://www.cmrc.on.ca/ProLifeIsrael welcome.htm

Web for Beth Yeshua: http://www.xs4all.nl/-byadam/

Publishes in Dutch: Life Line Uitgave van de stichting Beth Yeshua Nederland. Werkgroep Be'ad Chaim Nederland. Steit zich tot doel om het pro-life werk van Be'ad Chaim in Israël te steunen en gebed, financiën en medeleven. Tevens beoogt zij de Bijbelse visie op het leven in Nederland uit te dragen. Be'ad Chaim Centra zijn gevestigd in Jerusalem, Tel Aviv, Kfar Saba, Haifa en Tiberias.

C.D.L./Sendener Lebensrecht Tagungen (Right to Life Seminars)

Dr. Anneliese Funnemann
Holtrup 3, Schloss Senden
4403 Senden, Germany
Phone: +49.25. 97380
Fax: +49.25.976469

Catholic Family & Human Rights Institute
Austin Ruse, Director
866 United Nations Plaza, #4038
New York, NY 10017, USA
Phone: +1 212.754.5948 Fax: +1 212.754.9291
E-mail: austinruse@cafhri.com
Office E-mail: cafhri@cafhri.com
Website: www.cafhri.org

The Catholic Family and Human Rights Institute (CAFHRI) is a charity designed to serve the needs of United Nations delegates, extra-governmental and non-governmental organizations, missions and consulates, and those who have interests in life and family issues at the United Nations.

CAFHRI intends to fulfill an educational need to inform the public regarding family and human rights issues. Specifically, it will be an advocate on behalf of the rights and responsibilities of men, women and children, especially in relation to the family unit. Within this framework, issues such as population, development, and the environment will be addressed in support of present and future generations. They publish a weekly "Friday Fax" (that now goes by e-mail only) of the events at the United Nations. This covers issues on population control, family rights, environmentalism, and state sovereignty. They publish a monthly Newsletter - Vivant! with research articles to provide in-depth looks at life issues. Check out their web site for copies of Friday Fax and Vivant!

Care Ministries International
Mr. A. J. Ceelen, Executive Secretary
Van der Duyn van Maasdamlaan 2
3931 HR Woudenberg, Netherlands
Phone +31 33 286 3556 and Fax +31 33 286 3556
E-mail: ceelen@bigfoot.com
Website: www.kerk.net/cmi

This organization assists Jews to leave Russia and return to Israel and is active in human rights and pro-life activities.

Christians for Truth - Doctors for Life
Dr. Albertus van Eeden, MD
P.O. Box 61897
Bishopsgate 4008
South Africa
Phone: +27 31 306 0972 Fax +27 31 306 0958
E-mail: dewet1@x400.emg.co.za

Christian Life Family Church
Helping Hand Pregnancy Center
Phone: 321.953.2525
Luther Laite III, Pastor
4620 Lipscomb Street
Palm Bay, Florida USA 32905
Phone: 321.729.0000

Christian Life Family Church has spearheaded the closing of abortion clinics in the Melbourne, Florida area and has a crisis pregnancy center and other activities that support women and men with life issues decisions.

Christian Medical and Dental Society
Dr. David Stevens, M.D., Executive Director
P.O. Box 7500
Bristol, Tennessee USA 3721-7500
Phone: 1.888.231.2637

Health professionals in medicine and dentistry may wish to contact this group for information on membership and/or resources.

Coming Clean Ministries, Inc.
Dr. Jorge L. Valdés, Director
PMB 200
312 Crosstown Road
Peachtree City, Georgia USA 30269
Phone: 678.817.0749 Fax: 678.817.1862
E-Mail: jlvaldes@mindspring.com
Website: www.comingclean.net

This ministry assists people and other organizations dealing with drug-related problems, training, and teaching. Dr. Valdes is available for speaking engagements while not teaching at Seminary.

Concerned Citizens Christian Drug Prevention
Jkvr. E. de Marees van Swinderen, Esq., Secretary
Waalsdorperweg 285
2597 HX 's-Gravenhage, The Nederlands
Phone: +31.70.324.0523 Fax: +31.70.324.0523

Concerned Citizens, with international contacts, works directly with drug addiction problems on all levels in Holland and Europe.

Concerned Women For America
Beverly LaHaye, Founder (1979)
1015 Fifteenth Street, N. W., Suite 1100
Washington, D.C. 20005
Phone: 202.488.7000
E-mail: wwright@cwfa.org
(public relations representative)
Website: www.cwfa.org

CWA's mission is to protect and promote Biblical values among all citizens - first through prayer, then education, and finally by influencing our society, thereby reversing the decline in moral values in our nation. CWA has over 800 Prayer/Action Chapters and leaders in 49 states and over one half-million members nationwide, making CWA the largest public policy women's organization in the United States. We focus on the following six issues: Sanctity of Life, Religious Freedom, Defense of the Family, Pornography, Education, and National Sovereignty (including opposing our American government's attempts to implement any U.N. Global Plan of Action by either legislation or executive order by the President).

Coral Ridge Ministries
Rev. D. James Kennedy, Ph.D.
P. O. Box 407132
Fort Lauderdale, Florida 33340-7132

Coral Ridge Ministries Media, Inc. is Coral Ridge Ministries' pro-life, pro-family and evangelism branch with national radio and television outreaches. They have many materials available including their "Alert Bulletins."

The Counselor Corps, Inc.
Chris and Jean Sapp, Founders
505 Corinne Drive
Lehigh Acres, Florida 33936 USA
Phone: 941.368.7853
E-Mail: chrissapp@iline.com

Chris Sapp is an attorney and sidewalk referral counselor along with his wife Jean. They founded the organization to assist "reproductive referral counselors" (exact wording taken from the F.A.C.E. law), to be trained and loosely affiliated with REACH, their grassroots association of pro-life reproductive health service counselors. Using court decisions already reached by the U.S. Supreme Court (which affects all citizens regardless of state residence), Chris has formulated the permissible parameters of sidewalk counselors in the distribution of reproductive referrals (to pro-life doctors, and pregnancy counseling centers as alternatives to abortion). The decisions (Schenk and Scheidler cases, et al), clearly distinguishes between counselors and demonstrators, preachers, pray-ers, picketers, and others who enter into confrontations with clinic personnel. Call or write for information to organize in your area "under the law."

CREST Bangalore
Mrs. Dr. M.M. Mascarenhas, M.D.
East of NGEF-BDA Layout
Chikbanswadi, Bangalore
560016 India
Phone: +91 80 546 3076 Fax: +91 80 223 6671
E-Mail: roman.tellink@aworld.net

CREST is the pro-life initiative in India. Dr. Mascarenhas and her husband, Dr. Albert Mascarenhas meet many life issues needs but to the poor. They have special concerns for the plight of the girl-child and "burned" brides of India, and others are encouraged to learn more on these violations.

The Elliot Institute
David C. Reardon, Ph.D.
Post Office Box 7348
Springfield, Illinois 62791 USA
Phone: 217.525.8202
Order Line: 1.800.BOOKLOG
Web site: www.afterabortion.org

Dr. Reardon is the Director of The Elliot Institute and editor of their newsletter The Post-abortion Review that can be subscribed to by calling their order line. An expert in post-abortion trauma, he is the author of "Making Abortion Rare: A Healing Strategy for a Divided Nation", "The Jericho Plan: Breaking Down the Walls which Prevent Post-abortion Healing," and "Aborted Women - Silent No More." More publications are available. The Elliot Institute is a donor-supported, non-profit organization that does research and educates regarding the impact of abortion on women, men, siblings and society along with advocacy work on behalf of post-abortion outreach and healing. For extensive information on post-abortion issues, visit their web site.

Eternal Perspective Ministries
Randy Alcorn, General Director
Ron Norquist, Prolife Director
2229 E. Burnside #23
Gresham, Oregon 97030
Phone: 503.667.3013
E-Mail: epm@teleport.com

Fame Publishing, Inc.
820 S. Mac Arthur Blvd., Suite 105-220
Coppell, Texas 75019 USA
Phone: 972 393 1467 Fax: 972 462 9350
Toll-Free Order Line: 1.888.326.3782
E-mail: famepub@aol.com
Web site: http://hometown.aol.com/FamePub

Fame Publishing, Inc., publishes and distributes Christian books, software, gifts, and other products to proclaim Jesus Christ as Lord. Since beginning the company in 1990, their scriptural theme has been Luke 4:14. "And Jesus returned in the power of the Spirit into Galilee: and there went out a fame of him through all the region round about." America's God and Country Encyclopedia of Quotations by William J. Federer American Student's Package (CD-ROM by Christian Technologies); William J. Federer's American Quotations and Noah Webster's 1828 Dictionary

Family of the Americas
Mercedes Arzú Wilson, Founder
P.O. Box 1170
Dunkirk, Maryland 20754 USA
Phone: 301 627 3346 and 800.443.3395
Fax: 301.627.0847
E-mail: FAF@idsonline.com

Mercedes Arzú Wilson is the president and founder (1977) of the Family of the Americas Foundation, and founder of the World Organization for the Family. She has been a delegate to several United Nations Conferences and has authored articles, books, and Natural Family Planning programs. Wilson was appointed by Pope John Paul II, as a member of the Pontifical Academy of Life. Readers are welcome to call for additional materials in many languages; books, interactive CD-ROMs and disks that cover all aspects of fertility, natural birth control, family matters, teen sexuality and chastity. Their specialty is the Ovulation Method of Natural Family Planning with millions of couples in over 100 countries trained to use this safe and inexpensive birth control method.

Family Research Council
Gary L. Bauer, Founder
Robert L. Maginnis, Senior Policy Analyst
801 G Street, NW
Washington, DC 20001
Phone: 202.393.2100 Fax: 202.393.2134
Legislative Hot Line: 202.783.4663
Order line: 1 800 225 4008
E-mail: rlm@frc.org
Web: www.frc.org

Family Research Council is a Christian conservative organization upholding Biblical family values (including life issues) and monitors American legislative processes. It provides materials and updates on issues that guard families. They publish a monthly newsletter "Family Findings" which are topically written research papers. Call for materials.

Genesis Counseling
Joe Dallas
1774 N. Glassell
Orange, CA 92680
Phone: 714.502.1463

Educational materials by Joe Dallas on homosexuality and related issues are available through Genesis Counseling. For a free catalogue of the Genesis audio and video cassette series and for information on seminars by Joe Dallas, please contact him at the above address.

Genetic Engineering - A Christian Response: Crucial Considerations in Shaping Life
Timothy J. Demy and Gary P. Stewart, Editors (1999)
Correspondence: Publicity Department
Kregel Publications, Inc.
Post Office Box 2607
Grand Rapids, Michigan 49501

This book is highly recommended for those seriously considering in-depth Biblical answers to genetics and its place within the Christian community and the believer's heart. The revolution in science and medicine is nothing new and certainly one God foreknew. Hessel Bouma III observes in the foreword, "Like impatient pioneers, scientists blaze a path with genetic engineering on a frenzied race toward a better medicine, often with scant time to consult a moral compass."

The Global Society for Life
Mrs. Sharon L. Turner, Director-USA
105 Schweitz Road
Fleetwood, Pennsylvania 19522, U.S.A.
Phone: 610.682.1782 Fax: 610.682.1783
E-mail: Upwardcall@msn.com

The Global Society for Life represents life issues especially for the people of China and Asia. Of utmost concern is the plight of the Asian girl-child and the cruel suppression that destroys by choice, the female fetus. Both women and men suffer from forced sterilization and forced abortion in the family. Sharon's efforts are focused on educating about the "one child policy" of China and its ramifications for other nations. Drs. Bert P. Dorenbos is Executive Director, International Office.

Good Girl Doll and China Company
Sharon L. Turner, Co-Founder with Laurel T. Hughes
Phone: 610.682.1782 Fax: 610.682.1783
E-Mail: upwardcall@email.msn.com

This company provides authentic Chinese dolls and other articles to commemorate the plight of the Chinese girl-child. Since very few dolls with Asian features are available, this baby doll will bring the importance of treasuring Asians to all precious children. Please e-mail to order your doll. An Internet site is anticipated.

Healing Triad Talks
J. Ron Eaker, M.D.
2258 Wrightsboro Road, Suite 400
Augusta, Georgia 30904 USA
Phone: 706.733.4427
E-Mail: reaker@pol.net

Dr. Ron Eaker has written, "Holy Hormones – Approaching PMS and Menopause God's Way" (ISBN:1-57921-236-0, WinePress Publishing, PO Box 428, Enumclaw, Washington 98022: 1999). He also puts out a pro-life woman-oriented newsletter called "FLASHES," a quarterly review of health news, reports, and advances in the world of complementary medicine with a focus on women's health issues, all anchored to biblical wisdom and guidance.

Heartbeat International
Virginia A. Cline, Director
7870 Olentangy River Road, Suite 304
Columbus, Ohio 43235-1319 USA
Phone: 614.885.7577 Fax: 614.885.8746
E-Mail: support@heartbeatinternational.org
Web: www.heartbeatnational.org

Heartbeat News
Mrs. Dale O'Leary, Editor
Post Office Box 41294
Providence, Rhode Island 02940
E-Mail: heartbeatnews@compuserve.com

Dale O'Leary is a researcher willing to help others with particularly difficult to research areas. The Irving Bieber Memorial Library East Coast Branch, and NARTH have assembled volumes of material available to researchers. The material has been carefully organized and summarized. If you are interested in a particular topic, a list of available material can be e-mailed to you. Dale says, "I would be happy to discuss any research project or provide background for any article. I am very distressed to see so many of those who share our concerns either writing without facts or using incorrect information. Since the vast majority of information in our files comes from research by homosexuals and their allies, it is a very powerful weapon. Think of me as a supplier of ammunition in the battle for the family and for the very precious souls who are trapped by deadly lies." Dale is a staunch life issues activist, attends UN conferences and her latest book is: "The Gender Agenda - Redefining Equality," (Huntington House/Vital Issues Press: 1997). You may get this directly from Dale or at bookstore s ($13.25 includes shipping).

NARTH (The National Association for Research and Therapy of Homosexuality)
E-Mail: 74747.2241@compuserve.com

The NARTH Bulletin may be subscribed to . This organization disseminates free, periodic information regarding homosexuality (from a Christian perspective) via their e-mail network. Just make a request at their e-mail address listed above.

James L. Hirsen, J.D., Ph.D.
Correspondence address:
Huntington House Publishers - Editorial Department
P.O. Box 53788
Lafayette, LA 70505 USA
E-mail: comments@amerifree.com

Dr. Hirsen is an internationally recognized attorney. Renowned as a speaker on constitutional, government, and global issues, he has appeared on radio and television broadcasts across America and hosts his own radio program over the American Freedom Network called "America's Advocate". He is a professor at Trinity Law School in Orange County, California, teaching Public International Law and related law school topics. His latest book is "The Coming Collision - Global Law vs. U.S. Liberties."

Home School Defense Association
Michael P. Farris, Esq., President
17333 Pickwick Drive
Purcellville, Virginia 20132
Phone: 540.338.5600 Fax: 540.338.1952

Capitol Hill Office:
119 "C" Street, S. E.
Washington, DC 20003
Phone: 202.547.9222 Fax: 202.547.6655

Home School Legal Defense Association is an advocate for Family and Freedom. Call for materials and information.

Helpers of God's Precious Infants
Sister Dorothy Rothar, C.S.J.
The Monastery of the Precious Blood
5300 Ft. Hamilton Parkway
Brooklyn, New York 11219
Phone: 718.399.8166

Sister Rothar travels extensively internationally for the Catholic Church as a trainer in sidewalk referral counseling and has trained other groups as well. She is the Director of volunteers at the above given address.

International Committee of Catholic Nurses & Medical Social Assistants (C.I.C.I.A.M.S.)
Sir Richard Lai, International President
No. 24 Jalan SS 2/97
47300 Petaling Jaya, Malaysia
Phone: +6037.176136 Fax +6037.161259
E-mail: rlai@pd.jaring.my

International Justice Mission
Gary Haugen, J.D., General Counsel & Founder
Michelle Conn, Executive Assistant
P. O. Box 58147
Washington, D.C. 20037-8147
Phone: 703.536.3730 Fax: 703.536.3790
E-mail: ijm@ix.netcom.com
Website: www.ijm.org

Dr. Haugen worked in the civil rights division of the U.S. Department of Justice and was Director of the United Nations genocide investigation into Rwanda. He is currently

President of International Justice Mission. His book, Good News About Injustice (Downers Grove, IL ,InterVarsity Press:1999), is a blockbuster glimpse of how to bring justice to the nation in which you live.

International Right to Life Federation, Inc.
John C. Willke, M.D., President
1721 W. Galbraith Road
Cincinnati, Ohio 45239 USA
Phone: 513.729.3600 Fax: 513.729.3636
E-mail: lifeissues@aol.com

Dr. and Mrs. (Barbara) John Willke have been involved with life issues for decades. They hold conferences and training sessions across the world. Mrs. Willke is the President to the Ohio Right to Life Chapter. They produce a complete newsletter that can be subscribed to by contacting them.

The Jesus People Information Center
4338 Third Avenue
Sacramento, California 95817
Phone: 916.456.9085
E-mail: JesusPeople@juno.com
Web Site: http://www.mission.org/jesuspeople

The Jesus People is a life issues grassroots evangelistic organization engaged in foreign missions, nationwide prison ministry, street evangelism and help for the homeless. They support missions by giving and sending much free literature to many nations. Their newsletter is available and also produces pro-life articles.

J.I.A.L. Ministries (Jesus Is Always Lord)
Bill Dorman (John 13:34-35) "Chaplain777"
P O Box 1061
Buffalo, Missouri 65622-1061 USA
E-mail: Chaplain777@hotmail.com
Web site: www.geocities.com/Heartland/Bluffs/2779/

The above address is for prayer requests or godly advice about anything. Any letters written to the Chaplain or any other members of this ministry will be read and prayed over. Bill Dorman's main ministry is to prisoners behind bars and their subsequent readjustment in society. JIAL publishes free, daily E-mail meditations. To subscribe, contact the e-mail above.

LEARN
Rev. Johnny Hunter, Founder & National Director
P. O. Box 6357
Virginia Beach, Virginia 23456
Phone: 757.495.3475
Website: www.learnusa.org

Life Education and Resource Network (LEARN) is a network of Christian pro-life, pro-family advocates who are dedicated to protecting the pre-born and promoting traditional family values. LEARN was officially established in 1993, at the African American Pro-life Planning Conference in Houston, Texas, to facilitate a strong and viable network of African American and minority life issues and pro-family advocates.

LEARN focuses on education, resources (a library), and networking among African Americans, although they heartily welcome all life issues advocates. Four areas of present concern are: The sanctity of Life curriculum for African American churches; Library for the study of Genocide and Eugenics, African American community outreach program expos and conferences, and audio and video production with mass distribution. Rev. Hunter is much in demand as a speaker and facilitator.

Koinonia House
Chuck and Nancy Missler
P. O. Box D
Coeur d'Alene, Idaho 83816-0347 USA
Phone: 208.773.6310 Fax: 208.773.6312
E-mail: update@khouse.org
Web pages: www.khouse.org (user name: trends and access code: welcome) www.ChristianBooks.com. and, www.AudioCentral.com

Koinonia House produces a News Journal called Personal Update to track internationally trends with commentary. Chuck has long been involved with intelligence work within the U.S. government and is a computer expert. Chuck and Nancy both speak at conferences and their ministry has many materials, videos, books, tapes, and teachings on globalism and life issues.

Liberty Council, Inc.
Mathew D. Staver, President and General Counsel
P. O. Box 540774
Orlando, Florida 32854 USA
Phone: 407.875.2100
E-Mail: liberty@lc.org
Website: www.lc.org

Liberty Council is a nonprofit religious civil liberties education and legal defense organization established to preserve religious freedom. It produces The Liberator, a monthly newsletter. Mat Staver has argued a pro-life case in front of the U.S. Supreme Court.

Life Advocacy Resource Project, Inc.
Penny Pullen, Director
2604 W. Sibley
Park Ridge, Illinois 60068 USA
Phone: 847-823-1004

Life Coalition International
Rev. Keith Tucci, Founder
Dr. Pat McEwen, Ministry Coordinator
P. O. Box 360221
Melbourne, Florida 32936-0221 USA
Phone: 321.726.0444 Fax: 321.726.0509
E-mail: patatlci@phonetech.com
Web: www.lifecoalition.com

This is an extremely active life issues and human rights organization working on national and international levels. LCI was the primary organization working for the release and relocation of the Golden Venture Chinese refugees. Rev. Tucci is a widely respected speaker, trainer and facilitator. Dr. McEwen writes, travels and speaks on behalf of LCI.

Life Issues Institute, Inc.
Bradley Mattes, Executive Director
1721 W. Galbraith Road
Cincinnati, Ohio 45239
Phone: 513.729.3600 Fax: 513.729.3636
E-mail: lifeissues@aol.com
Website: www.lifeissues.org

LifeSavers Ministries
Tim and Terri Palmquist, Founders and Co-chairman
P. O. Box 40972
Bakersfield, California 93384-0972 USA
Phone: 661.323.2229
E-mail: LifeSaver@HisCommand.com
Web site: www.PureVision.com/LifeSavers

The Palmquists have been in active pro-life service since 1984. They run LifeHouse , a live-in location for women in need. Their radio ministry Voice for Life is heard over KHIS 800 AM, but as funds are provided, they wish to take it nationwide to become the "voice for the babies." They also train sidewalk referral counseling, speak, hold banquets for fund raising, care for their seven children and have a newsletter called In Touch with Life Savers. They welcome your inquiries.

Lithuanian Association of World Federation of Doctors Who Respect Human Life
Mrs. A. Saulauskiene, M.D., President
Liauksmino str. 5
2001 Vilnius, Lithuania
Phone: +3702.612529 Fax +3702.612529
Phone: +3702.415101

Mrs. J. I. Tartiliene, Vice President
Zirmunu str 101-82
2001 Vilnius, Lithuania
Phone: +3702.774268

Lithuanian Family Center
Ms. Roma Baguckaité , Administrator
Aukstaiciu 10
3005 Kaunas, Lithuania
Phone: +3707.208263
E-mail: family_center@kaunas.omnitel.net

Dr. Paul Marshall
C/O: Word Publishing
Dallas, Texas, USA
Order Line: 800.251.4000

Paul Marshall is Academic Dean and Senior Fellow in Political Theory at the Institute for Christian Studies, Toronto, Canada, and Adjunct Professor of Philosophy at the Free University of Amsterdam. He has testified on religious persecution before the Helsinki Commission of the U.S. Congress and lectured on human rights at the Chinese Academy of Social Sciences Beijing and in 15 other countries around the world. Marshall is author and editor of 12 books and booklets including, "Their Blood Cries Out - The Worldwide Tragedy of Modern Christians who are Dying for their Faith" (ISBN: 0-8499-4020-6). Human Rights Theories in Christian Perspective; Stained Glass - World Views and Social Science; Thine is the Kingdom - A Biblical Perspective on Government and Politics, and Labour of Love - Essays on Work. His columns in Christian Week won the Canadian Church Press Award for the best columns in 1991. His work has been translated into eight languages.

The Monastery of the Precious Blood
Msgr. Philip J. Reilly, Executive Director
5300 Fort Hamilton Parkway
Brooklyn, New York 11219
Phone: 718.853.2789

Father Philip Reilly is a courageous (and often jailed) advocate for the lives of babies and their families. They have training materials and trainers for national and international seminars. The ministry has this purpose: "Our purpose is to be faithful and pleasing to God, and we hope that this will save the physical lives of God's precious infants through the spiritual conversion of their mothers. . ."

National Conference of Catholic Bishops
Richard M. Doerflinger, Associate Director
Secretariat for Pro-Life Activities
3211 4th Street, N.E..
Washington, DC 20017-1194 USA
Phone: 202.541.3171 Fax: 202.541.3054

National Right to Life Committee - California Pro-Life Council
Brian P. Johnston, Executive Director
2306 "J" Street, Suite 200
Sacramento, California 95816, USA
Phone: 916.442.8215 Fax: 916.441.7508
E-mail: prolife@californiaprolife.org
Web: www.californiaprolife.org & www.nrlc.org

New South Wales Right to Life
Greg Smith, President
29 Rosen Street
Epping, New South Wales 2121
Australia
Phone: +612. 876.2843

Physicians Resource Council
C/O Focus on the Family
Dr. James Dobson
8605 Explorer Drive
Colorado Springs, Colorado USA
Phone: 719.531.5181 Fax: 719.531.3424
Order line: 800.232.6459

Physician Magazine (free to medical professions) is only one of many publications dealing with pro-life and family issues that Focus on the Family sponsors. A copy of Dr. Bernard Nathanson's recent book, "The Hand of God" (Colorado Springs, CO, Focus on the Family: 1999), may be obtained directly from them.

PsicoEthos
Priscilla Carriedo Martínez, M.D.
Celaya No. 9-C
Col. Condesa
México, D.F.C.P. 06100
Phone/Fax: +264 4592 and +511 0124

Operation Rescue
Philip (Flip) Benham, Director
P. O. Box 740066
Dallas, Texas 75374 USA
Phone: 972.494.5366
Website: www.orn.org

Materials and books may be ordered from the addresses above at "Resistance Press" and from Huntington House Publishers (P.O. Box 53788, Lafayette, LA 70505). "Operation Rescue has had a profound affect on America and pro-life people everywhere. Founder Randall Terry is "a wake-up call to the Church; confrontational, controversial, and communicates a message...desperately needed." Says Jay Sekulow, Chief Counsel, American Center for Law and Justice. Flip Benham's group carries on this important rescue work.

Operation Save Our Nation
Rev. Robert L. Schenck
601 Pennsylvania Ave. NW, Suite 900
Washington, D.C. 20004
Telephone: 800. 551.2930
E-mail: PRSchenck@aol.com

Population Research Institute
Steven W. Mosher, Founder
P.O. Box 1559
Front Royal, Virginia 22630 USA
Phone: 540.622.5252 Fax: 540.622.2728
E-mail: pri@pop.org
Website: www.pop.org

Priests for Life - Pontifical Council for the Family
Piazza San Calisto 16, Trastevere Section
Rome, Vatican City, Italy
Phone: +3906.6988.7243 Fax: +3906.6988.7272
Email: 107742.3332@compuserve.com
Website: www.priestsforlife.org

Father Frank Pavone, Director - USA
Jerry Horn, Sr. Vice President
5404 Hazel Court
Fredericksburg, Virginia 22407 USA
Phone: 504.785.4733 Fax: 504.785.6232
E-mail: JerryHorn@aol.com
Website: www.priestsforlife.org

Priests for Life is directed by Father Frank Pavone and is dedicated to using seminars for clergy and extensive networking between clergy and pro-life groups of all denominations.

Pro-Life Action League
Joe Scheidler, Executive Director
6160 N. Cicero Avenue
Chicago, IL 60646
Phone: 773.777.2900 Fax: 773.777.3061
Newsline: 773.777.2525

Pro-life Association of Zimbabwe
Mr. Bob Phiri, Director
P. O. Box CY 402
Causeway, Harare, Zimbabwe
E-mail: JenniferM@cfs.co.zw & FrancesT@cfs.co.zw

Pregnancy Resource Center
Kurt and Gayle Dillinger
415 Cherry Street, SE
Grand Rapids, Michigan, USA 49503
Phone: 616 456 6873
E-mail: kdill@pregres.org

Kurt has begun a movement to establish crisis pregnancy centers in Michigan and beyond, training people internationally to start up crisis pregnancy centers.

Raiders News Update
Thomas Horn, Editor
Phone/Fax: 503 463 5821
E-mail: editor@raidersnewsupdate.com
Web: www/raidersnewsupdate.com

Tom Horn is a profilic writer and researcher. Contact him at his web site or E-mail to subscribe to his concentrated newsletter covering everything from life issues to the occult.

Religion Today News Magazine
E-mail: editors @crosswalk.com

Appendix B

Human Rights Organizations

The following groups do significant work on the persecution of Christians. There are also many other human-rights organizations (both secular and religious) with diverse foci whose work touches on this issue.

Advocates International
7002-C, Little River Turnpike
Annandale, Virginia 22003
Phone: 703.6580070 Fax: 703.658.0077
E-mail: sam.ericsson@gen.org

Advocates takes a long-term approach to religious liberty, focusing on the education of lawyers, judges, and legislators around the world.

Amnesty International
322 Eighth Avenue
New York, NY 10001
Phone: 212.807.8400 Fax: 212.989.5473
E-mail: aimember@aiusa.usa.com
Website: http://www.amnesty.org

AI is a prominent international organization that monitors and advocates on behalf of human rights. Amnesty has worked for the release of people imprisoned for the peaceful exercise of their religious beliefs. It also reports on the persecution of religious minorities.

Cardinal Kung Foundation
P. O. Box 8086
Ridgeway Center
Stamford, Connecticut 06905 USA
Phone: 203.329.9712 Fax: 203.329.6415

Monitors religious liberty abuses against Catholics in China.

Christian Life Commission of the Southern Baptist Convention
901 Commerce, Suite 550
Nashville, Tennessee 37203-3696

An arm of the Southern Baptist Convention, America's largest Protestant denomination. Seeks to draw the attention of Baptists and others to religious persecution, and lobbies for changes in U.S. government policy.

Christian Solidarity International
U.S. Office: 1101 17th Street, NW
Suite 607
Washington, D.C. 20036 USA
Phone: 540 636 8907
E-mail: csiusa@rma.edu

An international human rights organization headquartered in Switzerland that works for persecuted Christians and other victims of oppression. Conducts relief work, fact-finding trips, and organizes campaigns on behalf of persecuted believers.

Coalition for the Defense of Human Rights Under Islamization
231 East Carroll
Macomb, Illinois 61455
Phone: 309.833.4249

Focuses on the situation of religious minorities in the Islamic world.

Commission on Security and Cooperation in Europe
("The Helsinki Commission")
234 Ford House Office Building
Washington, D.C. 20515-6460 USA
Phone: 202 225 1901
E-mail: csce@HR.house.gov

A U.S. Congressional commission established in 1976 to monitor and encourage progress in implementing the provisions, including human rights provisions, of the Helsinki Accords on East-West cooperation. Several staff members monitor religious liberty developments in the Helsinki countries.

Freedom House's Puebla Program on Religious Freedom
Director: Nina Shea
1319 18th Street, NW, 2nd Floor
Washington, D.C. 20036 USA
Phone: 202.296.5101 Fax: 202.296.5078

Freedom House is a national organization dedicated to strengthening democratic institutions. With the addition of the Puebla Program directed by human-rights veteran Nina Shea, the group now also gives special attention to religious freedom. In 1996, they published an excellent booklet on the persecution of Christians around the world, In the Lion's Den, updated in 1997 by Broadman & Holman Publishers.

Human Rights Watch
485 Fifth Avenue
New York, NY 10017-6104
Phone: 212 972 8400 Fax: 212 972 0905
E-mail: hrwnyc@hrw.org
Web Site: www.gopher://gopher.humanrights.org:5000/11/int/hrw

An independent international human rights organization conducting regular investigations of human rights abuses in about 70 countries around the world. It has produced several reports about religious rights abuses, especially in China.

International Christian Concern
2020 Pennsylvania Ave., N.W.
Suite #941
Washington, DC 20006
Phone: 301.989.1708 Fax: 301.989.1709
E-mail: icc@ids2.unline.com
Web Site: http://esoptron.umd.edu/icc/ics.html

An independent Christian organization that mobilizes grassroots prayer and activism on behalf of persecuted Christians around the world.

Iranian Christians International
P. O. Box 25607
Colorado Springs, Colorado 80936 USA
Phone: 719.596.0010 Fax: 719.574.1141

An evangelical organization that monitors the persecution of Christians inside Iran; works to help Iranian Christian refugees and does advocacy work with the U.S. Government.

Jubilee Campaign
U.S. Office: 9689-C Main Street
Fairfax, Virginia 22031 USA
Phone: 703.503.0791 Fax: 703.503.0792
E-mail: ann.buwalda@gen.org

The U.S. arm of this British-based Christian group conducts campaigns on behalf of human rights and religious liberty around the world. Write their e-mail to get the British headquarters addresses.

Middle East Concern
P. O. Box 295
Macomb, Illinois 61455

Publicizes oppression and discrimination against religious minorities, especially Christians in the Middle East.

National Association of Evangelicals
P. O. Box 28
Wheaton, Illinois 60189
Phone: 630.665.0500
E-mail: NAE@nae.net
Website: http://www.nae.net

A cooperative of approximately 42,500 evangelical congregations nationwide (USA) from 47 member denominations and individual congregations from an additional 30 denominations whose executive serves on the White House Advisory Committee on Religious Freedom Abroad. NAE's landmark, "Statement of Conscience Concerning Worldwide Religious Persecution" is available on the web.

Open Doors with Brother Andrew
U.S. Office: P. O. Box 2700
Santa Ana, California 92799

A large international, evangelical organization formed to help suffering Christians throughout the world. Members deliver materials to persecuted Christians, conduct training sessions for indigenous leaders, and work to mobilize and educate churches to become more involved in helping persecuted Christians. It now publishes an informative newsletter called, "Compass Direct". Call for European headquarters information.

Compass Direct News Service
P. O. Box 27250
Santa Ana, California 92799 USA

A highly informative newsletter on the persecution of Christians, published by Open Doors.

Parliamentary Human Rights Foundation
1056 Thomas Jefferson Street, NW
Washington, DC 20007

This foundation is increasingly employing technology, specifically the Internet, to promote human rights internationally. Having parliamentarians from various countries on its board of directors, it seeks to pressure governments, which have the main responsibility to enhance human rights.

The Rutherford Institute
P. O. Box 7482
Charlottesville, VA 22906-7482
Phone: 804.978.3888 Fax: 804.978.1789
E-mail: rutherford@fni.com
Web Site: http://www.rutherford.org

An international legal and educational organization "dedicated to the preservation of religious liberty, the sanctity of human life, and family autonomy." The bulk of their work is on US cases, but they have a growing international division focusing on religious persecution around the world, especially in Latin America.

Voice of the Martyrs
Richard Wurmbrant, Founder
P. O. Box 443
Bartlesville, Oklahoma 74005 USA
Phone: 918.337.8015 Fax: 918.337.9287
E-mail: vomusa@ix.netcom.com

Website:
www.http://www.iclnet.org/pub/resources/text/vom/vom.html

Non-profit missionary organization working with persecuted churches in more than 50 countries around the world. Provides practical assistance to oppressed Christians and informs Christians in the West about ongoing religious persecution.

World Evangelical Fellowship Religious Liberty Commission
U.S. Office - 2309 139th Street, S.E.
Mill Creek, Washington 98012
Phone: 206 742 7923
E-mail: WEFNA@XC.Org
Website: http://www.xc.crg/wef/wefintro

This Singapore-based World Evangelical Fellowship is an umbrella group of evangelical associations worldwide and draws together some 180 million people from over 100 countries. From its main office in Finland, the Religious Liberty Commission coordinates the work of its members on issues of religious freedom.

Citizens Commission on Human Rights (CCHR)
International Headquarters:
6362 Hollywood Blvd. Suite B
Los Angeles, California 90028 USA
Phone: 323.467.4242 & 800.869.2247

Citizens Commission on Human Rights (CCHR)
David Figueroa, Director in Florida
305 N. Fort Harrison Avenue
Clearwater, Florida 33755
Phone: 800.782.2878

This human rights activist organization is funded by the United States International Association of Scientologists and deals primarily with the damaging path of psychiatry and psychology abuse. Their mandate is, to investigate and expose psychiatric abuses of human rights. "In the course of our 26-year history, we have researched psychiatric abuses in many forms all over the world including Australia, USA, United Kingdom, Germany, Italy and Bosnia and worked with government officials, politicians, law enforcement officials and health departments to effect changes."

Appendix C

Global Networking

One of the most powerful of all our tools in these technological days is the instant use of e-mails and the Internet. We have ease of communication like never before. The Bible talks about knowledge being widespread in the last days.

This would surely include the multitudinous electronic means of television, radio, cyberspace, digital science, and microchip inventions by which communications move through the air to outer space to satellites and then are beamed back in a different location. We watch live war on TV now. Of course, the old-fashioned ways are still practical. You can't send packages through the Internet. You've got to use snail mail!

Here is some excellent advice from a new friend, Dave Domingo, to expand our effectiveness through the use of electronic mail and the Internet for pro-life causes.

Networking Globally by E-mail and the Internet

As a newspaper copy editor and a freelance copy editor for book publishers, I spend a lot of time communicating and doing research on the Internet. I also have put a lot of energy into my own pro-Jesus, pro-life Web site.

I would like to share some advice about using the Internet as a tool for pro-life communication. Unfortunately, this message will be a bit long, which flies in the face of my first point:

A. Keep e-mail messages short.

As a rule, use e-mail to alert people, but use Web pages to educate them. E-mail messages should include just a brief summary of what's new and to give links to applicable Web pages. This is good advice for at least three reasons:

(1) People like to make choices. When I open a long message, I feel pressured to read the whole thing right then—but I really enjoy getting a nice, brief message on a new development with a link to a Web page where I can get all the details. I can choose to click the link and get into the material at a time that's good for me.

(2) Linking to existing information (yours and other people's) is less time consuming than re-expressing it in a message.

(3) And, most importantly, sending short messages with no attached files shows consideration for the recipient. Many users (think global) have slow hardware and have to pay through the nose, by the minute, for their Internet connections. Others are just very busy and get annoyed at having to download files they may not want. You may want to tell them you have more information if they are interested.

B. Take advantage of free resources.

Don't pay for anything you can get for free. I have free Internet access and a free e-mail account through NetZero, free Web-site hosting through *Homepage.com* and a free fax-to-e-mail service through efax. (I get no payoffs from any of these companies.) The cost of NetZero is having a free-floating ad banner (advertisement) layered on top of my screen the whole time I'm connected, hoping I might buy from them.

The cost of Homepage.com is that a *Homepage.com* banner appears at the top of all my pages. But the advantage of using Homepage.com instead of another free hosting site like Tripod is that Homepage's URLs are simpler.

Would you rather tell people you are at, "members dot tripod dot com slash tilde wordshop," or simply say, "wordshop. homepage.com"? And the cost of efax is borne by the people who send faxes long-distance to my assigned number at efax. (Efax then sends the faxes to me as e-mail.)

The company makes its money by letting clients upgrade to a toll-free service for about $30 a month.

C. Don't reinvent anything.

If you have something new to say, say it, but don't waste energy echoing what someone else already said really well. Summarize and link to them. For example, on my anti-abortion page, I don't tell people much about pregnancy centers, the legal history of abortion, pro-life activism or Planned Parenthood's roots in Nazi-style eugenics.

Instead, I link to Pregnancy Centers Online; the Barnes & Noble listing for my dad's book, *Orphans in Babylon* (Roger Domingo); the Pro-Life Action League; and the American Bioethics Advisory Committee or the Family Research Council.

Using Internet Links

Next to each link, I give clear but brief explanations of what the links go to and why the user should go there. I also have links for hard-to-find gems like the "Baby Hope" columns by Mona Charen, the "Surrender of the Left" essay by Jim Trageser, and a speech by Alan Keyes about the discussion America never had on abortion. I definitely could not have said those things better myself, so I linked to the originals.

Like a good speech, a good site gives people the motivation and a means to *do* something.

For example, on my site I urge users to circulate copies of the Hippocratic Oath at medical school graduation ceremonies and to suggest to the graduates that they read it during the ceremony instead of the watered-down, pro-abortion version they probably have been issued by their school. I also link to another page on my site where users can read and print the oath. That's a call to action and a tool!

I pray that these tips will help readers take better advantage of the blessings of electronic communication.

—Dave Domingo

Here are a few more tips for using the Internet and creating a Web site to get a response and bring attention to your message.

1. You can make smart use of chat rooms, allowing you to address several people at once who are in that chat room. Using "real time," you can get more done than stopping to shoot off an e-mail over and over again.

2. In designing your Web site, it helps to be self-effacing. For example, you will get more feedback from a button labeled "Click here to criticize our site" than from one labeled "E-mail us with your comments."

3. Frequent Internet users have found that you are three times more likely to get people to respond to you by engaging them in an e-mail conversation than if they simply read through your Web site. So make it easy for them to connect with you in several places if possible.

4. Be careful on the Internet. All is not always what it seems. Establish your list of pro-life organizations and contacts and make inquiries for those you do not know. Legitimate people will be happy to answer your questions.

5. E-mail. Check out messages that come to you from people you do not know, especially the "forwarded" ones. Go to the source or do some research. Be very, very careful about just passing information on that seems unusual, exploiting, exaggerated, or hurtful. Your own reputation will suffer when you constantly pass on gossip or non-information. And who has time for that?

Get Free Resources

One of the best things to do is to get connected with a free e-mail service, meaning one that uses advertising every time you boot up but does not charge for long-distance connections. These will be different in various parts of the world. Juno is one such service that can be found on the Internet, but there are others.

Get a quick reference guide like *Internet: Find It Faster Because You Read Less* by David Gosselin. This one tells you about the Internet, the global collection of computers, and computer networks. It tells you the history, how to connect, and how to access major resources. There are also many free resources available in public libraries.

Don't be discouraged about getting on the Internet. If you are not ready to do that (or never will be), your e-mail capabilities are wonderful to use and keep the Word circulating on life issues. So is snail mail!